"*Neighborology* is an excellent resou ... . Drawing from more than thirty years of experience in diaconal and mercy ministry, Dr. David Apple gives biblically based, practical advice about loving our neighbors. If you serve in the church as an elder or deacon, this book will help you greatly in your ministry to the sheep of your fold. I recommend this book for anyone who works in mercy ministry, and especially those who will serve as officers in the church of Jesus Christ."

—Mark Casson
Director of Prison Ministry, Presbyterian Church in America

"In *Neighborology*, David Apple again contributes uniquely to literature on mercy ministry by telling vivid stories. The stories prove that biblical mercy ministry is possible and profitable for ordinary churches and saints! Here, as followers of Jesus, we learn in concrete ways, by precept and example, how to listen and speak to our neighbors. Addressing racial tension develops as one theme of the book; the specific instructions to help congregations work through those matters alone is worth the purchase price."

—Rev. James Faris
Reformation Society of Indianapolis

"The Lord Jesus told us the second greatest commandment is, 'Love your neighbor as yourself' (Matt. 22:39). In this wonderful book, Dr. Apple has provided an amazing tool to teach the church to be neighborly with the mind of Christ. Following the gems contained in this precious jewel will result in His church reflecting the love of neighbor which our Savior commanded and modeled, especially as it relates to believers loving one another across racial barriers. I highly recommend this book."

—Ray Hutchison
SIM USA East Central Regional Director

"*Neighborology* challenges and corrects our view of discipleship and missional engagement as it calls us to live out what it means to be a gospel-driven, Christ-centered neighbor. My friend David Apple illustrates how Jesus entered into the lives of the least, the last and the lost by engaging with them as the perfect neighbor. He then charges us to leap into the lives of those in need with care, concern and godly stewardship. This is an invaluable tool for churches of every ministry context. Get it! Read it! Live it! Preach it!"

—Rev. Doug Logan
Lead Pastor, Epiphany Fellowship, Camden, NJ

"With personal, practical and biblical insight, David Apple has given us a book that helps us see what it looks like when we obey Christ's command to love our neighbors as ourselves. While not denying the difficulties, he guides us into urban as well as suburban neighborliness in such areas as hospitality, visitation and shepherding. I recommend this to all Christians ready to bridge the divisions that separate us sinners from our neighbor sinners around us."

—Mary Beth McGreevy
Adjunct Professor, Covenant Theological Seminary

"In *Neighborology*, following on the heels of *Not Just a Soup Kitchen*, Dr. Apple seeks to shed further light on the biblical motives behind being a good neighbor and the implications for taking seriously our Lord's command to love our neighbor as ourselves. Without any hint or suggestion that mercy ministry is easy, Dr. Apple prods us toward a new obedience of denying ourselves, taking up our cross and following Jesus, exhibited in that loving concern for and compassion toward our neighbor. It would be difficult to come away from this book without a renewed zeal to serve others, armed with both the theoretical and the practical."

—David P. Nakhla
Administrator, Committee on Diaconal Ministries
for the Orthodox Presbyterian Church

"David Apple's *Neighborology* not only shows that a true love for God will produce practical love for our neighbors, it also shows that Christ's welcome of us resources our hospitality and reminds us of our need to be received by and learn from our neighbors. Whether you are part of a small group that needs to exercise your service muscles or a ministry veteran who needs a refreshing cup of cold water, this book will prove valuable."

—Dr. Gregory Perry
Associate Professor of New Testament
& Director of the City Ministry Initiative, Covenant Seminary

"A very helpful guide for local churches seeking to develop or expand their ministry to needy neighbors. Solid biblical foundations. Practical, concrete advice. *Neighborology* grows out of several decades of successful holistic ministry leading a large, center-city, evangelical congregation into greatly expanded ministry with their most neglected neighbors."

—Dr. Ronald J. Sider
Distinguished Professor of Theology, Holistic Ministry
and Public Policy, Palmer Seminary at Eastern University

NEIGHBOROLOGY

NEIGHBOROLOGY

PRACTICING COMPASSION
AS A WAY OF LIFE

Dr. David S. Apple

PUBLICATIONS

Fort Washington, PA 19034

Neighborology
Published by CLC Publications

U.S.A.
P.O. Box 1449, Fort Washington, PA 19034

UNITED KINGDOM
CLC International (UK)
Unit 5, Glendale Avenue, Sandycroft, Flintshire, CH5 2QP

© 2017 David S. Apple
All rights reserved. Published 2017

Printed in the United States of America

ISBN (paperback): 978-1-61958-239-2
ISBN (e-book): 978-1-61958-240-8

Cover design by Mitch Bolton.

THIS BOOK IS DEDICATED TO

all the men and women who have heard the call of God
to love their neighbor.

To those who are ordained, "Thank you."

To those who are commissioned, "Thank you."

To those who are anointed, "Thank you."

I also thank my colleagues at Tenth Presbyterian Church
who encouraged me and prayed for the fruits of this book.

And, most of all, I thank my dear wife and friend, Kate,
for her sacrificial love during the writing of this book.

To all those capital "D" and lowercase "d" deacons,
"I praise God for you."

"To him who sits on the throne and to the Lamb be
blessing and honor and glory and might forever and ever!"
Revelation 5:13

CONTENTS

INTRODUCTION

S oon after I received the contract for this book, a book that was supposed to be about "developing the heart of a servant," I had a week filled with stress. Many extremely needy people came in to see me or called me on the phone. Some were emotionally challenged or had some type of mental illness. The bulk of them were people who had no appointments. Yet it was important that I see them all, and it was important to them that they see me. Most who phoned were locals, but a few were from distant states. (I still wonder: Why do they call me?) When I came home from serving at Tenth Presbyterian on the last workday of that week, I announced to my wife, "I no longer want to be a mercy minister. I want to be a ship builder!" I wanted to bang things, make lots of noise, and, for a change, have a finished product as a result.

I knew from experience that there would be what I call the "satanic attacks" of interruptions, disruptions and discouragements. But I suppose that I didn't expect attacks like these. Oy vey! Welcome to the world of mercy ministry!

Full-time mercy ministry is sacrificial. The essence of the ministry is listening to Christ's call to "follow Me." My needs are secondary. As a mercy minister, I have said to God, "Not my will, but thine, be done" (Luke 22:42, KJV). I have picked up my cross and followed Him (see Mark 8:34). I have sought to crucify the flesh daily (see Gal. 5:24). None of these acts have come easy. I do not like being submissive. I do not like giving up the right to have my own way. But the good news about these particular weaknesses of mine is that they bring me to the foot of the cross on a daily basis.

One of the things I've learned in over twenty-five years of directing Tenth Presbyterian Church's mercy ministry is something I call "prayerful patience." In my early years there, I was impatient to start ministries, and I sometimes used the Bible to bludgeon people with ideas about what needed to happen now. I was in the fast lane looking for even more speed, but I was dealing with a three-miles-an-hour God. I gradually learned the discipline of "active waiting" and came to put my trust in the transforming power of the Holy Spirit instead. In time, God rose up other mercy-minded leaders, and Tenth Church now supports a spectrum of fruitful mercy ministries and mercy ministers. In time, Scripture states, you will "bear fruit—fruit that will last" (John 15:16, NIV). This promise sustained us all in its show of mercy and compassion.

The relational approach to evangelism is rooted in Christ's model of incarnational love and sacrificial servanthood. Jesus became a servant of others, washing their feet and not being afraid to be vulnerable with them. He came alongside people who were hurting, those who may have smelled or otherwise made others uncomfortable.

We are also called to be advocates, to come alongside people and be available to them. Serving is a means for us to be available to people, knowing that God is in charge of the timetable.

Evangelism and discipleship are central to mercy ministry. If someone has no friends, has no support, he or she is likely to feel abandoned and hopeless. They might feel alienated from themselves, others and God. They might even say to themselves: Why bother? But when we peel away the layers of need, the greatest craving is spiritual, so there must be a spiritual solution. The starting point for renewal is spiritual. It's only with Christ that people possess the freedom to finally look beyond themselves for a source of healing.

Decades ago, when Tenth Church faced the decision of whether or not to sell its property and move to the suburbs (where there was lots of grass and parking), we could have followed the trail of so many other urban churches. However, the congregation decided to remain. We stayed, not to keep our beautiful building, but to be Christian witnesses in serving our neighbors. The church website proclaims, "This church opens wide her doors and offers her welcome in the name of the Lord Jesus Christ."[1]

Here's the bottom line: Our goal in welcoming is not to "win converts," but to make disciples. When Jesus said, "Go and make disciples of all nations," (Matt. 28:19, NIV) He meant that His followers' lives would be totally, unconditionally submitted to Him. This submitting is a lifelong process—a once-in-a-lifetime choice that takes a lifetime to accomplish. It is one thing to say that Jesus saved us from our sins. It's another thing to say that He is our Lord and owns everything that we have. Mercy ministry is as much about bringing Christians to a deeper commitment of discipleship as it is about serving those outside of the church. Part of mercy ministry is converting uncaring church members into church members who have compassion for the unwanted and unlovely—the widow, the orphan, the beggar and the addicted. God desperately wants these church members to share His concern for the broken and brokenhearted.

This book follows my book *Not Just a Soup Kitchen: How Mercy Ministry in the Local Church Transforms Us All*.[2] It provides a further blueprint for how the church—the people of God—can be the neighborly helpers God intended and, especially, how we, as helpers, can serve smarter and more effectively. I desire for church leaders to envision the future: What do we want our churches to look like in five or ten or twenty-five years? Do we want the next generation of our congregations to act and look the same as we do today? What transformation is needed and what will it take to achieve it? What differences do we want to make in the lives of those who sit in our pews? What differences do we want to make in the lives of those who live in and around our neighborhoods? What trainings do we want for our deacons and members?

Neighborology, as a book and a concept, considers the following themes: the development of servant hearts, every-member ministry, the ministry of hospitality, and volunteerism. It also describes how to set safe boundaries so we do not become rescuers, that is, how to deal with difficult people and how to prevent "compassion fatigue" and burnout. These are areas of concern that most pastors never learn in seminary and that deacons and other church members are rarely taught.

Through this book, I hope to encourage churches to shift or tweak their ministry paradigms in order to raise up future generations of servant-leaders. I hope to help deacons work "outside the box" instead of in the "we've always done it this way" mode of operation. And I will share various stories, pilgrimages, trials and other experiences that will benefit readers and their churches. By the end of this book, my hope is that each reader will have developed a servant's heart and a new understanding of "neighborology."

1

A THEOLOGY OF CARING

I call her Mary. I've never met her and I don't know her real identity. She has left me over fifty voice mail messages in the last year. She usually calls in the middle of the night when I'm not in my office. Each time she does, she shares her difficulties with life—how no one cares about her, and how she does not like one particular neighbor who is a church member. I would really love to speak with "Mary," but her phone number comes up as anonymous. I have yet to be able to track her down, speak to her and tell her I care.

BEING MADE NEW

Really caring about other people is hard work. It is beyond challenging. This is true for me and, I believe, for all of us. That is, until we become more like Jesus through spiritual regeneration and transformation. Regeneration, or being made new, means that we turn over to God all dependence or allegiance we have to people, places or things. We submit to God all addictions, habits or attempts to please people instead of Him. This process of transformation is God leading a holy war in our lives, as He did in Deuteronomy 7, where anything belonging to the opposing gods must be totally destroyed. Regeneration, transformation and renewal, then, have to do with who is in charge of our lives. It means that we must please God above all others.

Personally, I have a prideful hunger to be appreciated. I have been a people pleaser most of my life. As a result, I am in a continual process of allowing God to be the focus of who I am and what I do—moving beyond just knowing about Christ to knowing Him personally and knowing that I am loved by Him unconditionally. It is also important for people pleasers like me to spend quality time with God.

Jesus often took time out to spend time with His Father, and He often retreated to a quiet place (see Mark 1:35; Luke 5:16). What set Jesus apart was His intimacy with God, which denoted a close, loving and trusting relationship with the one he called "Abba." Jesus was a person of prayer. The busier He got, the more He turned to God in prayer. Why? Because He knew God! He understood God as a loving Father whose main interest was to love, teach and heal His people.[1]

To know God is to have the same relationship with Him as Christ does. The difference is that we are sinful and need forgiveness. Biblical counselor Larry Crabb states in his book *Encouragement* that sometimes he is afraid of God and expects anger. "As I await the pronouncement of my well-deserved rejection, I hear his loving words and see his loving smile. And I am eternally encouraged for he has spoken from his love to my fear."[2] The biblical truth is that God loves us; and although we—in our sinful nature—are worthy of rejection, He has forgiven us and adopted us as His children.

FINDING SOLITUDE

Our relationship with Christ comes from His journey with us and our pilgrimage in life's wilderness—climbing proverbial mountains and learning to find joy and contentment as God transforms our lives. Even though God's love for us has remained unchanged, our love for God often runs hot and cold and lukewarm.

This is certainly true for me. Like the apostle Paul, I often don't do the things I know I should be doing and do the things I should not be doing (see Rom. 7:15–20). At times I have been fearful and frightened, feeling worthless or without value. I have felt alienated from people and from God: afraid to reach out and distrustful of those reaching in. This is why I must find more and more solitude with God—and also why I am so afraid of it.

In his book *Reaching Out,* the late Roman Catholic theologian Henri Nouwen describes how most of us fear being alone and, therefore, fear solitude.

> Our lifestyles are vehicles for anesthesia. Panic occurs when we have run out of distractions and are brought close to aloneness. The lonely, hurting, suffering people reach out to momentary, illusory experiences, self-deceits that say "now everything will be better." People desire more and more receive less and less. We need a journey of the spiritual life.

> We must find the courage to enter into the desert
> of our own loneliness and by gentle and persistent
> efforts change it into a garden of solitude, from
> restless energies to a restful spirit, from outward
> cravings to inward searching.[3]

Yes, the process of discovering what Nouwen calls "entering the desert" is a risky one. It requires that we commit ourselves to that solitude where spiritual lives are formed. Out of this solitude, we find a new calmness of spirit, a freedom from old, negative and locked-into patterns of feeling, thought and action. This process uncovers the very being of our souls. It exposes us and makes us vulnerable to God Almighty. It makes us participate in becoming known by God. Acknowledging our sin, pain and brokenness is part of true repentance and confession. Yet, as difficult as this process is, we don't go through it alone; the Holy Spirit empowers us step-by-step to place our burdens on Him (see Matt. 11:28). And as we learn to care for ourselves, we are more able to care for and be good neighbors to others.

Solitude also makes intimacy possible. We must, through solitude, empty ourselves of self and listen to what God is saying to us about making room for others. Yes, solitude is very much connected to our work as ministers of mercy! It deepens our affection for one another: we are free to love one another because God first loved us. In moving from loneliness to solitude, we are able to move from anxious reactions to loving responses as we are transformed by Christ and His forgiveness. True repentance comes from a Spirit-led desire to change. It sets us free and leads us to worship and service.

This new freedom leads us from a lifestyle of caring less to a lifestyle of caring more, from hostility to hospitality.

HOSTING

Our freedom in Christ's love is a commitment to serving others. While loneliness promotes hostility, anger and fear, solitude makes us good hosts. According to theologian Henri Nouwen, "A good host is one who believes his guest is carrying a gift he wants to reveal to anyone who shows genuine interest. A good host shows encouragement, affirmation and support and welcomes the contributions of others."[4] We are called upon to be hosts, providing hospitality and creating space for others. As followers of Christ, we offer safe places where we can welcome strangers and where healing and growth can take place.

I love the example of hospitality that Jesus provided us: "While we were still sinners, Christ died for us" (Rom. 5:8). Hospitality allows us, as Romans 13:14 says, to "put on the Lord Jesus Christ," meaning that we have the mind of our Savior. We then turn our *hostis* into *hospis*,[5] as Nouwen says, putting away all hostility and bitterness, and making others better than ourselves (see Phil. 2:3). This change in attitude draws us away from old selfish patterns and leads us to imitate Christ. With this change, we are then aware of our neighbor's needs and begin to love them as Christ loves us. Before my Christian conversion, if someone on the streets came up to me and asked for something to eat, I would reply, "Get out of here you bum." Now if a homeless person says they are hungry, I might offer my sandwich or a piece of fruit and, if I have time, will sit and talk with him. When we imitate Christ, we model His humility, submission and service (see Phil. 2:1–12). The power of the Holy Spirit enables us to take action for God's sake. Humility frees us to do the will of God. We become free from serving ourselves to serving others. In humility, we submit ourselves to serve God and neighbor without demanding anything in return. Submission allows us to value those whom God brings to us. Nouwen calls these people God's gifts.[6]

I'm reminded of a church member who had plans to go out with some of his buddies. On his way to meet them, he came across a neighbor who was "down and out" and in need of help. The church member immediately contacted his friends to cancel and took his neighbor to the nearest Christian rescue mission. In the name of Jesus, he gave up the right to have his own way for the sake of someone else.

SERVING OTHERS

In serving others, we again seek to follow Christ's example. He came not to be served but to serve (see Matt. 20:28). If you're like me, saying "No" to helping others is easy. Learning to say "Yes" is a discipline that must be exercised.

In *The Spirit of the Disciplines,* Christian philosopher Dallas Willard states:

> We engage our goods and strengths in the active promotion of the good of others and the causes of God in our world. [We] may also serve others to train ourselves away from arrogance, possessiveness, envy, resentment or covetousness. In that case

service is undertaken as a discipline for the spiritual life. Service is the high road to freedom from bondage to other people. We cease to be "manpleasers," for we are acting unto God in our lowliest deeds.[7]

That kind of attitude comes from a relationship with Christ. "We serve out of whispered promptings, divine urges" of the Spirit,[8] says spiritual director Richard Foster in *Celebration of Discipline*. All service is important. There is no measurement that distinguishes between small and large service. Those with servant hearts are content to serve in "hidden" ways, with no need for recognition. They serve for God's honor and glory. Foster continues:

> True service is indiscriminate in its ministry. It has heard the call of Jesus to be "servant of all." True service ministers simply and faithfully because there is need. It refuses to allow feelings to control service, but rather the service disciplines the feelings. True service is a life-style. It acts from ingrained patterns of godly living. True service can withhold the service as freely as perform it. It can listen with tenderness and patience before acting. It can serve by waiting in silence. True service builds community. It puts no one under obligation to return the service. It draws, binds, heals and builds.[9]

Service to others requires a need for constant renewal. As God transforms us to become more like Jesus, we learn what it means to be clay in the hands of the Potter.

We learn the meaning of the hymn, "Have Thine Own Way, Lord."

> Have thine own way, Lord! Have thine own way!
> Thou art the potter, I am the clay.
> Mold me and make me after thy will,
> While I am waiting, yielded and still.[10]

An auto accident in 1982 put my life on hold. I was in constant pain, unable to work, with no income and no idea what the future looked like. Suddenly, I was in the hands of the Potter, trusting, waiting, "yielded and still."

FURTHER GROWTH

The spiritual growth I found in being yielded and still was not through the performance of religious rituals, but by developing a dynamic relationship with Jesus Christ. In the four years I was unable to work, I sought to strengthen that relationship through daily Scripture reading and prayer. The fruits of that experience were enormous. Before my accident, I had posted "no trespassing signs," thinking I could prevent God from molding and shaping me according to His will. But this was foolish. The best action I could take was to willingly surrender to God. Looking back, I can see that God used this experience to mold me into His image.

Around the same time, I began to have flashbacks of being sexually molested as a child—a memory I had unconsciously buried to protect myself. Each time the flashbacks occurred, I attempted to bury the memories once again, but they continued to resurrect themselves. I felt so broken and I could not fix myself. My brokenness was all for good. God was at work. By understanding God's love and sovereignty and the limitations of my own timetable and agenda, I gained peace. But change took time and the power of the Holy Spirit. It required patient waiting. Similarly, God was waiting for me to pray for the work of the Spirit, to fill me with His presence, His thoughts and His words.

Speaking on this type of spiritual renewal, God's love in us must be visible. If people don't see in us a walk and a talk that reflects holiness, that is a good indication of where we are spiritually. God's love is seen as we live it out. Our relationship with Christ must have an impact on all our other relationships: spouse, children, friends, employees, employers. There is no relationship that you and I can enter into that is not directly affected by our spiritual life in Christ. Servant hearts are shaped by our spiritual lives in Christ, and the result is our serving the world around us. When we study the Bible, we should have ears to hear what God is saying to us—words that mold us to be good neighbors.

Spiritual renewal should make us more conscious of our relationship with God: how he cares for us and how we must care for others because of this loving relationship. This is what I call a "theology of caring." This theological mind-set is born from our personal pilgrimage involving a search for identity and the development of a healthy relationship with God the Father and Jesus Christ, His Son.

It also involves developing a godly, obedient understanding of service and caring. Having this biblical theology of caring empowers us to live out the great command to love the

Lord with all our hearts and to love our neighbors as ourselves (see Matt. 22:37–39). We who have servant hearts are molded and perfected as God changes us over time.

> Consider it pure joy, my brothers, whenever you face trials of many kinds, because you know that the testing of your faith develops perseverance. Perseverance must finish its work so that you may be mature and complete, not lacking anything. (James 1:2–4, NIV)

This character building is essential for those whom God uses as His compassionate servants and good neighbors.

BECOMING PEOPLE OF COMPASSION

The character we need for caring is found in Jesus and the power of our resurrected Savior. We are then able to consciously and consistently model His love and do what does not come naturally, that is, minister selflessly, serve with compassion, seek the welfare of others and love our enemies.

Only by personally knowing Christ's love and concern are we able to care for others. It is by His "breathing" in us that we are once and forever changed. We move higher and deeper into meaningful relationship with Him, with His help.[11] In this relationship we know and enter into His care and compassion and become part of His incarnated ministry through us on Earth. His heart of compassion asks us to come alongside those in need. In his book *The Search for Compassion,* theologian Andrew Purves says, "Compassion asks us to go where it hurts, to enter into places of pain, to share in brokenness, fear, confusion, and anguish. Compassion challenges us to cry out with those in misery, to mourn with those who are lonely, to weep with those in tears."[12] He says that we need to be people of compassion who will not be too quick to take away pain, but will have the spiritual and mental toughness to walk alongside another, sharing in their journey to the point where woundedness can be confronted.[13]

Compassion is hands-on ministry that requires servant hearts. It demands love. Compassion is ministry without limits. It is evangelical, bringing persons to a place where they may "taste and see that the Lord is good" (Ps. 34:8). Purves writes:

> Compassion is the ministry of Jesus Christ by which he enters into another's brokenness. Compassion is situational. It cannot be pre-packaged. Compassion is vicarious. It means suffering with another. Compassion bridges the gap between social and pastoral ministry. Compassion demands a spiritual relationship with Jesus Christ. This final descriptor is the most vital element in that it makes compassion possible and is found whenever people are being liberated to serve, where they search after a faithful and obedient walk.[14]

Our faith and our compassion is a biblical demonstration that Jesus is the Lord of our lives.

Questions to Consider

1. What role has solitude played in your spiritual growth? How have you watered the "desert" of your soul?

2. How has God transformed your character? What was the experience like?

3. Describe an experience where God changed hostility into hospitality.

2

DEVELOPING THE HEART
OF A SERVANT

What is the process for developing the heart of a servant? Jesus is very clear: "Whoever loses his life for my sake will find it" (Matt. 10:39). "If anyone would come after me, let him deny himself and take up his cross and follow me" (Mark 8:34).

Having the heart of a servant lies in the concept of victory through loss, a commitment to following Jesus. If we will not do things the way Jesus says, He tells us we are not worthy of Him (see Matt. 10:37). Our Lord requires us to ask, "What can we give?" This is in stark contrast to postmodern Christianity, which asks, "What do we get?" His requirements for us are costly.

One illustration of this occurred years ago when I worked for government as a social worker. I kept a Bible on my desk when meeting with a client. It was my practice in many cases to ask if I could read Scripture and pray for them. If the client gave me permission, I would read and pray. If not, I would not.

Over the years, my atheist supervisor warned me to stop this practice because it violated "church and state." My response was always, "As a Christian, I can't *not* do it" because it would violate my Christian beliefs. Finally, after repeated "offenses," I was told that I should quit or be fired. I quit. Being a faithful servant and disciple of Christ cost me my job.

The cost of discipleship is seen many times throughout the Gospels. Luke 14:25–27 states that we must hate our father, mother and our own lives to serve Jesus Christ. The meaning here is that if we say Jesus is Lord and is first in our lives, then we must love everyone close to us less than we love Him—not to hate per se, but to rank second, third, etc. When Jesus begins Matthew 16:24 with the words, "If anyone would come after me," He is speaking about a complete and total surrender. In Luke 9:23, Jesus adds the word "daily" to emphasize that He is calling us to an everyday lifestyle of obedience to Him. Jesus' utterances remind us of the three attitudes we must have when we come to Him: self-denial, cross bearing and Jesus following.

DENYING OURSELVES

What is self-denial? It means that we decide to leave self behind and that in every moment of life we say no to ourselves and yes to God. Church of Scotland minister William Barclay (1907–1978) said:

> To deny oneself means once, finally and for all, to
> dethrone self and to enthrone God. To deny oneself
> means to obliterate self as the dominant principle

of life, and to make God the ruling principle, more, the ruling passion, of life.

To deny ourselves is . . . to ignore the very existence of oneself. It is to treat the self as if it did not exist. Usually we treat ourselves as if our self was far and away the most important thing in the world. If we are to follow Jesus, we must forget that self exists.[1]

In his *Commentary on the Whole Bible*, eighteenth-century pastor Matthew Henry says that self-denial is no more than what Jesus practiced to redeem and instruct us and is, also, the fundamental spirit required for admission into Christ's school.[2] It is the sum and substance of Christ's call to true discipleship, coupled with daily taking up the cross and following Him.[3] But we Christians struggle as we attempt to deny ourselves. Living godly lives in service to the church and our neighbors is difficult and troublesome. It is also thoroughly and completely opposed to the practice of our secular society. Who in his or her right mind would want to live a life of self-denial?

After my conversion, I transferred from a junior college to attend Calvin College. My proposed roommate decided at the last minute to attend a different school, and I was alone in my dorm room. Sometime afterward, I noticed another student, Albert, who roomed by himself. No one wanted to room with him or even be with him because he was such a difficult person. No one wanted to come alongside of him and be a good neighbor either. Because of this, I met with the dean of students and asked for permission to room with Albert.

Permission was granted, and I learned firsthand how difficult and troublesome he was. Yet God provided sufficient grace for the both of us, and each of us grew spiritually.

SELF-DENIAL TO MOST IS DEVIANT BEHAVIOR

To most of the world, my actions would be labeled "deviant" behavior. Yet in Jesus' kingdom, the King acts as a servant, and He makes his kingdom known by serving those who suffer. Values that are considered normal (i.e., paying little attention to those with great need) are changed to show that the law of God is to love one's neighbor. The meaning of life is no longer centered on self-interest. The law of Christ motivates us to give our lives to Him and to others. This new law on our hearts encourages us to ask what we can do to help others. Unfortunately, according to Gerald Schlabach in *And Who Is My Neighbor?*, "we have been trained to believe that fulfillment comes to those who make their lives an endless round of party going with plenty of laughs. But Jesus tells us that people who cry because their hearts are broken over the things that break the heart of God are the fulfilled people in this world."[4] To the world, that is certainly deviant behavior.

Deviance implies that there is some action that goes against cultural norms and expectations. But, there are sociological distinctions. A behavior or condition may be normal or abnormal, moral or amoral, depending on the culture. What is normal in one culture may be deviant in another and vice versa.

Christians represent a self-denying culture. In Christ, self-lessness is a badge of identity. Those who are in Christ, and who have become disciples of Christ, show by their actions that they are following Him.

A volunteer on our staff befriended a homeless drug addict and, over time, spent many hours speaking with him and counseling him. The volunteer continued his contact and visitation even after the addict was convicted of a crime and sent to a distant prison. When the ex-convict returned to Philadelphia several years later, our volunteer was there to help him again.

SELF-DENIAL IS COSTLY

Jesus' teachings present the world with a new model for living: self-denial. The road to joy is found in compassionate living for others. Can you imagine Jesus saying to His disciples, "Take up your cross and follow me—it'll make you feel good"? Of course not. But to some people, the idea of denying self is absurd. When our ministry staff goes on an outing, they invite our poor and homeless neighbors and spend the day strengthening relationships and caring for some of their needs. This has included trips to the National Aquarium in Baltimore, Phillies baseball games, the Jersey Shore and elsewhere. Many times we have had to pray for wisdom when responding to specific needs, but self-denial is not easy. It is neighborly, loving and the right thing to do.

Jesus showed us that love can be painful and costly. His service on our behalf certainly was not cheap. He gave His life! Therefore, our service in Christ for others must cost us something as well. Having servant hearts requires a great investment on our part.

Dietrich Bonhoeffer, a Lutheran minister who died at the hands of the Nazis in 1945, challenges us to embrace a costly grace.

> Costly grace is the gospel which must be sought again and again, the gift which must be asked for, the door at which a man must knock. Such grace is costly because it calls us to follow, and it is grace because it calls us to follow Jesus Christ. It is costly because it costs a man his life, and it is grace because it gives a man the only true life. . . . Above all, it is costly because it cost God the life of his Son: "You were bought with a price," and what has cost God much cannot be cheap for us. Above all, it is grace because God did not reckon his Son too dear a price to pay for our life, but delivered him up for us. Costly grace is the incarnation of God.[5]

To embrace this costly grace is essentially a conversion to and an invitation to follow Jesus. This conversion to self-denial begins first in the mind. We cannot serve others until our minds are freed from the world's influence and then transformed by the Lord's power. Conversion is an invitation to develop servant hearts and, through that process, be used by God for the sake of others. God converts us to His love not only as a means in itself, but also to the end that we will offer His love to others. I mentioned earlier in this chapter how I was led at Calvin College to room with Albert, a very unlikable person. In the two semesters we shared the dorm room, we also played ball and did many other things together, apart from others. I know looking back, that this sacrificial service greatly benefited Albert and glorified God.

SELF-DENIAL REQUIRES A RESURRECTED MIND

"When Jesus calls a man," according to Bonhoeffer, "he bids him come and die."[6] Those who have a heart for God—servant hearts—must go by a way that is sacrificial. For Japanese theologian Kosuke Koyama, to have a heart for God is to "read the scriptures with [others'] needs in mind."[7] He says that the essence of having a heart for God is having the mind of Christ. It is allowing Emmanuel, God with us, to influence our lives today through the salvific work He accomplished. The mind of Christ is therefore "the resurrected mind." His victory over the grave guaranteed our salvation. His resurrection made it possible for us to have a resurrection mind-set and a biblical worldview. The servant heart begins with the nurture of the resurrected mind. According to Koyama, "There is no way to domesticate Jesus Christ."[8] Doing so would distort the image and power of God. Too many times we give God our intellectual compliance while refusing to turn over our wills and agendas to Him. Jesus surrendered His entire will to do the will of His heavenly Father.

In Christ we have been called to surrender and summoned to lay down the burden of self-will. We can then fall freely and totally into the arms of Jesus, trusting Him completely for all things for all time. This is part of what the apostle Paul speaks about when he says, "I have been crucified with Christ and I no longer live, but Christ lives in me" (Gal. 2:20, NIV). We need to be crucified—purged of everything that cannot be used by God—so God can raise us up for use in the world. God attached Himself to the world in order to produce the crucified and resurrected Savior and, in the Savior's followers, a resurrection mind-set. This means that, as Christians, we attach ourselves to the needs of others. Many cultures would oppose this belief system. For example, in Thailand, being detached represents the idea of good. It is portrayed for Thai people as "clothing washed, neatly ironed and placed in a closed, undisturbed drawer. Don't wear it! It will get dirty! The clothing must stay detached from the dirty world."[9] This detachment is a commitment to noninvolvement.

Similarly, many Christians neatly store biblical teachings on helping the poor and needy in their own tightly sealed boxes. They do not practically apply the parable of the good Samaritan (see Luke 10:25–37) or Jesus' teaching that we love Him when we show mercy to others (see Matt. 25:35–40). I see this lack of mercy ministry in churches all over the United States.

Too many Christians want to keep their Bible teaching undisturbed in a drawer, neatly ironed, always clean and untouched. But Jesus calls us to be committed and attached to our neighbors and their suffering.

A few years after I began serving at Tenth Church, and as our mercy ministry grew, more and more of our homeless neighbors began coming to Tenth not only for meals, clothing, counseling and fellowship, but also for worship and Bible study. I remember one member saying, "You should do this ministry in North Philly or Kensington. This is a church, not a mission." In spite of such attitudes, we continued. Over the years, lives have been changed, and captives have been set free—those on the street and those in the church pews. In my estimation, very few Christians truly follow Jesus in ministry to the poor, to the outcast and to other vulnerable people. They don't seem to be interested in outreach, only in becoming more learned. They seem to be content sitting in the church pew, unscrewing the tops of their heads to have Bible information put in, and then screwing the tops back on tightly so the information does not leak out.

But our neighbors are not interested in our Christology. They are most interested in our being . . . well . . . neighbors. They are not concerned with whether or not we love God with all our heart, soul, and mind (see Matt. 22:37). They are concerned with our self-denial and whether we love our neighbor as ourselves (see 22:39). Our neighbors can very easily explain the passage, "He who does not love his brother whom he has seen cannot love God whom he has not seen" (1 John 4:20). I am reminded about a friend's story concerning a needy woman. She frequently stood on a street corner near his church singing the song, "Do not pass me by." Yet, all those who saw her did pass her by. They enjoyed her singing, but did not see her neediness. Jesus was not like this. Christ, facing the reality of his neighbors' needs, accepted the claims His neighbors made on Him. Our attitude toward our neighbor, modeled after the likeness of Jesus, carries with it a unique responsibility for theological and practical obedience to Jesus. The only way we can be authentic in our lives and lifestyles is by imitating Christ in our personal relationships like a friend of mine. He did not pass the woman by, but again and again returned to her and established a relationship. He invited her to the evening church fellowship dinner; and when she finally accepted the invitation, he introduced her to a female staff member who became a friend. Over time, the woman received the help she needed, joined the church and sang in the choir.

WHAT WE NEED TO SEE

How sad it is when the church fails to show it cares. In *Outgrowing the Ingrown Church*, church planter and pastor Jack Miller says, "I was standing in the midst of the Great American Church Tragedy. That tragedy is the local church with an abundance of resources and spiritual gifts held back by unbelieving apathy."[10] The chief reason for this apathy is that "needy" people—the sick, the dying, the poor and the despairing—are usually not attractive, and sometimes they have fallen into their problems through their own efforts. It is easy for Christians to start looking for the noble, deserving poor and to discover that such people are in very short supply.[11] We are all undeserving. We need to educate ourselves about those to whom many basic needs are denied. This is not the kind of learning that is done for its own sake, as if it were enough to know about poverty and be against it. Rather, it is a kind of education that serves as a catalyst. It is intended to lead to other kinds of activity and to give meaning and purpose to those actions. Learning about poverty is one thing. It certainly helps us to understand the nuances and complexities of those who are living in those situations. But establishing relationships with people who live in poverty is an entirely different level of engagement. Being involved in and with the poor is a prerequisite to caring for and helping them in many ways. The Bible calls us to learn about and care about others (see Matt.

25:40; 1 John 3:17; Phil. 2:4). Former Congressman Ernest Hollings tells what this kind of learning meant to him.

> I was a victim of hunger myopia. I didn't really see hunger until I visited some families in a Charleston, South Carolina slum. Before we had gone a block, I was miserable. I began to understand that hunger is real, that it exists in hundreds of humans in my own home city. I saw what all America needs to see. The hungry are not able-bodied men, sitting around drunk and lazy on welfare. They are children. They are abandoned women, or the crippled, or the aged. Bridging the barrier of economic segregation and becoming acquainted with the poor near our own homes might do more to help us understand what Jesus and the prophets were talking about than anything else we could do.[12]

At Tenth Presbyterian Church, we seek to establish relationships with our neighbors, particularly those who are poor or homeless, through thrice-weekly meals and small-group Bible studies. In addition, we continue to call on our church members to develop servant hearts, as we lead them to serve in these ministries and establish relationships with their neighbors.

These relationships establish opportunities for greater ministry and help our neighbors grow in Christ and gain skills for independent living. Here, neighbors and church members grow spiritually as the Scriptures are read, explained, understood and put into practice. Here, Christians are growing, joyful in giving of themselves for the benefit of others. Here, people are learning to follow Jesus.

TAKING UP OUR CROSSES

In early first-century Rome, each condemned criminal was forced to carry his own cross-piece to the place of crucifixions. Condemned men hanging on their crosses was not an uncommon sight. After the revolt following the death of Herod the Great, the historian Josephus recorded that two thousand Jews were crucified by the Roman proconsul Varus.[13] Jesus' disciples understood the full meaning of the cross.

By taking up our crosses, we are committed to killing off our old selves. The *Word Biblical Commentary* says, "To take up one's cross means a deliberate dying to oneself, modeling a lifestyle patterned after the example of the Master."[14] We can no longer place any hope in ourselves, or in anyone or anything else. The apostle Paul says that we cannot belong to Christ Jesus unless we crucify all self-indulgent passions and desires (see Gal. 5:24). We are called to accept our deaths— that in the cross, the "self" of us has been brought to an end. When we understand this fact, we are ready to follow Jesus.

A personal, consistent self-denial is part of the Christian walk. The way of the cross is Christian discipleship. We say to God, "We will do it your way." Real crosses involve surrendering our will and our use of time and money for the benefit of others. For example, some of us would do anything else rather than spend time studying Scripture and praying. Others of us might find taking opportunities to share our faith burdensome and so avoid them. Bearing real crosses means saying yes to some important things for Jesus' sake.[15] Bearing real crosses means all the things mentioned in Matthew 25:35-36—feeding the hungry, satisfying those who thirst, welcoming the stranger, caring for the sick and visiting the prisoner—and feeding, satisfying and caring for our own spiritual needs as well.

Every week, Tenth Church volunteers meet with homeless neighbors, welcoming them into the church building for Bible study followed by a meal. These volunteers could be doing anything, but they sacrifice their time for our guests. One volunteer established a friendship with a guest and provided him much help, including temporary residence in his own home.

Essentially, taking up our crosses means accepting whatever God has given us or made us and then in priestly fashion offering it to Him as our "reasonable service" (Rom. 12:1, KJV).[16] This is the cross of the Christian life: Having received from God, we gladly offer everything back to Him.

WE ARE PRIESTS

Our priesthood is rooted and grounded in Jesus alone. He is the Great High Priest whose priesthood was not ordained by man but, rather, was ordained by God. The author of the letter to the Hebrews says about Jesus, "You are a priest forever" (Heb. 5:6). He continues in chapter 7:

> Such a high priest meets our need—one who is holy, blameless, pure, set apart from sinners, exalted above the heavens. Unlike the other high priests, he does not need to offer sacrifices day after day,

first for his own sins, and then for the sins of the
people. He sacrificed for their sins once for all
when he offered himself. (7:26–27, NIV)

The apostle Peter compares us to our High Priest when
he writes, "You also, like living stones, are being built into
a spiritual house to be a holy priesthood, offering spiritual sacrifices acceptable to God through Jesus Christ" (1 Pet.
2:5, NIV). He also says, "And do not forget to do good and
to share with others, for with such sacrifices God is pleased"
(Heb. 13:16, NIV). We are called to build one another up by
giving and living for others as Jesus did.

As our eternal High Priest, Jesus offered Himself on the
cross once and for all time. As the only sacrifice acceptable
to God the Father, Jesus cleansed us from sins, freed us from
guilt, restored our relationship with God and redeemed us as
His people. But Scripture does not simply teach us that our
High Priest died on our behalf; it also teaches us that, because of His death, we have been made priests in Him. The
same Priest "who loves us and has freed us from our sins by
his blood," also "made us [to be] a kingdom, priests to his
God and Father" (Rev. 1:5–6). Thus, our benefit from Christ's
priestly office is to be a royal priesthood. God proclaimed
that those who walked in obedience to His covenant would
be His "own possession," a "holy nation" and a "royal priesthood" (1 Pet. 2:9). The doctrine of the priesthood of all believers made it possible for Christians to reclaim a character-
istic that previously had been given only to ordained priests.
This doctrine teaches that all Christians are priests and that
as priests, we serve God—no matter what vocation we pursue.

An article by David Hagopian says this about the priesthood of all believers:

> There is no vocation that is more "sacred" than any other. Because Christ is Lord over all areas of life, and because His Word applies to all areas of life, nowhere does His Word even remotely suggest that the ministry is "sacred" while all other vocations are "secular." Scripture knows no sacred–secular distinction. All of life belongs to God. All of life is sacred. All believers are priests.[17]

According to Martin Luther, priesthood has its privileges, but these are of task, not of rank. Luther says, "All believers have equally received the treasures which God has given, from the shoemaker to the farmer to the smith. No vocation stands over and above the rest. God has called all believers, without exception, to be His royal priests."[18] There is no legitimate vocation too low to be the vehicle through which God will do His work. In his "Treatise on Good Works," Luther also said that the most important of all good works is faith in Christ. To the question asked in John 6:28 (NIV), "What must we do to do the works God requires?" Luther answers, "'This is the work of God, that ye believe on Him Whom He hath sent.' . . . For in this work all good works must be done."[19]

Similarly, the *Belgic Confession of 1561* states that Christians cannot help but do good works.

> We believe that this true faith, produced in us by the hearing of God's Word and by the work of the

Holy Spirit, regenerates us and makes us new creatures, causing us to live a new life and freeing us from the slavery of sin. . . . So then, it is impossible for this holy faith to be unfruitful in a human being, seeing that we do not speak of an empty faith but of what Scripture calls "faith working through love," which leads people to do . . . the works that God has commanded in the Word.[20]

Thus, because Christian priests are this new creation, they do good works through the power of the Holy Spirit. The Gospel of Luke tells us, "So you also, when you have done all that you were commanded, say, 'We are unworthy servants; we have only done what was our duty'" (17:10). Martin Luther concludes, "So a Christian . . . does everything cheerfully and freely; not that he may gather many merits . . . but because it is a pleasure for him to please God thereby."[21] I am reminded of an early job opportunity I had in my hometown of Paterson, New Jersey. Because of my mother's political connections, I was offered the position of welfare department director, a position that would have brought much prestige and income. At the same time, a caseworker position was available that would allow me to experience every possibility of coming alongside people, spending time with them and providing both help and hope in Christ. I happily took the caseworker position.

WE ARE PART OF A NEW REFORMATION

Out of our gratitude then, we participate in God's mission: He has told us to take up our crosses and to "go therefore and make disciples of all nations" (Matt. 28:19). Christianity is a movement of the laity, that is, the people of God. Jesus' missionary calling was given to all who believed. Mission belongs to the entire church and those men and women who both believe and practice that principle. The greatest need in churches today is that church leaders train, motivate and mobilize the people of God for ministry. Every member is valuable. No member is useless. Every member has received talents to be used in the service of others.

Our gifts and our service are to be used for the benefit of others and not to serve ourselves. In his book *The New Reformation*, Greg Ogden states that our royal priesthood "seeks nothing less than the radical transformation of the self-perception of all believers so that we see ourselves as vital channels through whom God mediates his life to other members of the body of Christ and to the world."[22] The church is God's reconciling presence in the world. We are a community of gifted and talented priests who have denied ourselves and have taken up our crosses. It is in this new identity as crossbearers that we are able to imitate Christ in the world. God enables all Christians to serve Him as royal priests who follow Him, serving others. I see this in so many of our mercy ministry staff but especially in one woman who retired several years ago. She retired from forty years of paid employment, but she volunteered to service of others. Every Tuesday she takes the bus to the local prison to serve those "serving time."

The apostle Paul says in Romans 12:10 (NIV), "Be devoted to one another in brotherly love. Honor one another above yourselves." And in Philippians 2:4 (BSB), "Each of you should look not only to your own interests, but also to the interests of others." Putting others first is a cross we must bear. Jesus Himself is the model we must follow.

FOLLOWING JESUS

Both the Old and New Testaments contain the idea that believers are those who follow God in trust and obedience. For the Hebrew nation, it meant obeying the law and the prophets. New Testament believers were commanded and encouraged to follow the Lord's commandments and the principles of faith that came from the apostles and from Christ Himself.

Jesus still speaks the same two words, "Follow Me." For us, following Jesus still means leaving everything behind. Following Christ is becoming united with Christ, and in doing so, we repeat the marriage vow, "Forsaking all others, as long as we live." In Him, we have a new identification and a command to act as He did. The apostle whom Jesus loved wrote, "Whoever says he abides in him ought to walk in the same way in which he walked" (1 John 2:6). As Jesus' disciples, we follow Him by living lives of active obedience. When we were children, we played a game called "Follow the Leader."

No matter what the leader did, we had to follow his or her steps. Now that we are adults and have put away childish things, our Christian walk consists of following—in thoughtful, loving, obedient steps—our divine leader Jesus Christ, who modeled for us self-denial, cross bearing and following in a continual awareness of the demands of God and the needs of others. Since 1988, Tenth Church has had many ministry interns who have chosen to work in the area of mercy. Their hope has been to achieve knowledge and wisdom for a life committed to ministry to, for and with hurting men and women. Each of them has shadowed me and others and has followed our lead as we seek to reproduce ministers of mercy. Following Christ implies learning how He loved. Following Christ means being neighbors.

WHO IS OUR NEIGHBOR?

As our minds become more and more like the mind of Christ, we become increasingly sensitive to the needs of those around us. Whether we agree or disagree, God's truth is that anyone in need is our neighbor. We must replace the question "Who is my neighbor?" (which restricts our response) with "Whose neighbor am I?" (which liberates our response). Theologian Kosuke Koyama says, "One cannot know beforehand whom he will meet. The immediate sight of a neighbor demands a spontaneous answer. One becomes a neighbor, also, to people outside one's group, nation, or race."[23]

Similarly, Calvin College's Lester DeKoster says in *The Deacons Handbook*:

> Why waste time discussing how we will know who our neighbor is? Just go and be "neighbor" to someone, to anyone, in need. Let the needy find his neighbor in you. Drop the talk. Cut the chatter. Take God's gifts of time, money, goods, talents, counsel, a listening ear, a helping hand . . . out there where someone can use them. To love your neighbor as yourself means simply to be a neighbor whenever and wherever you can.[24]

The person in need is the one whom God places in our path. His or her need may be big or small, physical, emotional or spiritual. It may be obvious to all, or obvious only to those who can see through the person's mask or cover-up.

In the Gospel of Luke, Jesus tells the parable of the good Samaritan to make clear to His listeners who their neighbor is. The familiar story tells of a Jewish man who was beaten, robbed and left for dead. Those who passed by were aware of his injuries and need but ignored them. The Jewish priest had religious reasons: If the body had been a corpse, and he touched it, he would be unclean for seven days (see Num. 19:11). The Levite, a temple worker, would not take any risks to help either. To these religious officials, law and ceremony were more important than love and the suffering of others.

The Samaritan, however, the one Jewish people despised, was prepared to help—he risked his safety and altered his schedule to become involved with a needy person of another race and social class. I often tell the story of how a group of black teenagers befriended me. I was a high school student who, because of childhood injuries and abuse, was emotionally and physically crippled and without hope. They made it their business to come alongside me for the long run and to minister to my needs. The result, three years later, was my coming to faith in Christ. Like the Good Samaritan, they understood how to be good neighbors.

WELCOMING AND FORGIVING

Jesus lived a life of submission to the Father. He gave up the right to have His own way. He surrendered the right to retaliate and gave up the right of having "sweet revenge" against His enemies. His submission was seen in His ability to forgive His oppressor-neighbors: As He was being crucified, Jesus said, "Father, forgive them, for they know not what they do" (Luke 23:34). Jesus' submissive attitude allowed Him to love others unconditionally. Neighbors were a reality for Him. He saw worth and value in the needy people He encountered, which is the opposite of what most people—even Christians—do. In our own minds, we keep "those people" at arm's length, making them peripheral beings, sometimes even worse. We often speak as if such people do not exist as humans. Our perception is that people only have worth if they possess what the world values: money, property and fame. I have heard people say, "I am not my brother's keeper" when given some responsibility to help others. Their body language—a shrug or a frown—indicates to me that, to them, "those people" are not worth it.

In spite of whether or not people have possessions, Jesus knows the worth of all humankind, and He demonstrated a unique self-denial to His neighbors by bearing His cross and walking obediently before His Father.

For Jesus, service was not merely performing service tasks or giving money, but being a servant. It was a deliberate, conscious statement of who He was and who we should be as we follow Him. Jesus showed us that life is a gift that is not to be possessed, but shared. He showed us that hospitality involves receptivity. We must gladly welcome the stranger in. Jesus' love of His neighbors flowed out of an inward sense of love, joy, peace and obedience. Our motive for loving our neighbors is gratitude to God for His eternal, unchanging love for us.

The heir of the Borden Dairy Corporation, William Borden, was considered "royalty" as his family had wealth. For his high school graduation, they gave him a trip. While on the trip, he began to feel a burden for those less fortunate. He returned to America and enrolled at Yale University where he started a Bible study; founded a mission for those who were on the streets of New Haven; and shared the gospel with orphans, widows, the homeless and the hungry, offering them hope and refuge.

When Borden graduated from Yale, he entered Princeton Seminary and, upon graduation, set sail for China intending to serve Christ there. Along the way, however, he contracted spinal meningitis and died soon after. When his Bible was discovered after his death, six words were found written on the inside page: "No reserve, no retreat, no regrets."[25] Denying self, he gave up his earthly wealth to follow Jesus and serve those in need.

Denying self, taking up the cross, and following Christ describe three different ways of living for God and others. As a community of people who deny themselves, take up their crosses, and follow Christ, we are called to live in radical opposition to the powers of evil, showing forth a new way of living. Tenth's mercy ministry is made up of many, many people who sacrifice their time, talent and resources to love their neighbors. These neighbors live on the street, in shelters, in "abandominiums," in nursing homes and in prisons. They are all either brokenhearted or broken down from experiencing much hardship in their lives.

A recent phone call from one of my ministry coordinators reminded me of the powers of evil that are against us.

Commenting on a Sunday Bible study with our homeless neighbors, he listed three times in ninety minutes where there were spiritual attacks. These disruptions from just one guest included false gossip about a leader, a physical threat against another guest and a personal threat against the coordinator himself. How should the coordinator respond? It is our calling to live out the communal life in radical obedience to the One who is our model.[26] Our modeling Christ is evidence that as good neighbors we have the hearts of servants.

Questions to Consider

1. What "cost of discipleship" have you incurred?

2. Describe an experience where you gave up the right to have your own way? What caused your response? How did that make you feel?

3. Comment on the quote, "Let the needy find his neighbor in you." What goes through your head?

3

A NATION OF GIVERS?

While still aboard the ship Arabella, John Winthrop, the first governor of the colony of Massachusetts, encouraged his people to bear one another's burdens, practicing the Christian duty of love, rather than looking only to their own concerns. He said, "We must delight in each other, make others' conditions our own, rejoice together, mourn together, labor and suffer together, always having before our eyes our commission and community in the work, our community as members of the same body."[1] In signing the Mayflower Compact, the Pilgrims pledged, "to all care of each other's good and of the whole by everyone and so mutually."[2] In essence, all were to deny themselves, take up their crosses and follow Jesus.

On his visit to the United States in 1835, Alexis de Tocqueville observed that a voluntary cooperation—a spirit of generosity and helpfulness toward our neighbors—was deeply ingrained in the American heart. "If an accident happens on the highway," he wrote, "everybody hastens to help the sufferer."

And, he observed, "If some great and sudden calamity befalls a family, the purses of a thousand strangers are at once willingly opened and small but numerous donations pour in to relieve their distress."[3]

For centuries, in American cities and towns—whether segregated, integrated, urban, suburban or rural—people's responsibilities to the poor, the stranger, the hungry, the family and the community were carefully defined by social norms reflective of biblical standards. In our day, these absolutes of providing care have waned in importance. Although most churches I've visited across the United States help those in need, many have given that responsibility over to the government, parachurch organizations and private associations. In some abstract sense, we still feel that we should help the needy. But, as a nation, we do not have the same social pressure that tells us we should show compassion or be compassionate people. According to missiologist Ray Bakke, many churches are split into what is known as either "truth" or "love" churches (or, as I would call them, "mercy" churches).[4] The "truth" churches preach the gospel of Jesus Christ and people's need for salvation on Sunday but show little evidence of mercy and compassion throughout the week. The "mercy" churches teach little about sin and salvation but are rich in good deeds.

Today, almost two centuries after de Tocqueville, substantial numbers of people fear that they cannot count on others for help, especially if they become seriously ill. According to a survey conducted by Robert Wuthnow of Princeton University, 37 percent of people feel they cannot count on their immediate neighbors and 36 percent think they cannot depend upon church or synagogue members for help. Yet when asked about the importance of helping people in need, 73 percent say it is absolutely essential; another 24 percent say it is fairly important. Only 2 percent say it is not very important. [5] What a paradox there is when a large percentage of people feel they cannot depend on others for help, and at the same time, a similarly large number believe that helping others is important.

VOLUNTEERISM

A large number of Americans are volunteering. According to a study by the Independent Sector, 93 million Americans volunteered more than 20 billion hours in one year. This averages out to 218 hours per volunteer. [6] But, as Pastor Eugene Rivers of Boston's Azusa Christian Community asked, "If there are really 93 million volunteers in America, then why are our cities worse than they have ever been?"[7] The answer to this question is that more than one-fifth of those hours consists of informal volunteering—anything from babysitting for friends to baking cookies for school fundraisers. These figures also include volunteers at cultural institutions and those who serve on boards and committees. [8]

The same pattern prevails in churches where volunteer hours are more likely spent nurturing the church family and maintaining the church building, while few hours are spent reaching out to the needy. "Volunteerism, Christian-style, is much more likely to mean serving on the parish council or the vestry, not conducting Life Plan seminars in prison," says Roberto Rivera of the Wilberforce Forum, a ministry of Prison Fellowship. "In the current volunteer economy," he adds, "giving the Metropolitan Opera $10 million . . . is [counted] the same as using that money to help 3,000 inner city kids attend private schools. Changing that economy requires reinventing human nature and that's not going to happen. The seeming generosity of American people is often an expression of self-interest. In caring for others, we care for ourselves."[9] I know many people who give to the arts above all else because these institutions provide them with much pleasure as well as a tax deduction.

In the article "Do Do-Gooders Do Any Good?" Michael Gerson says that only 8.5 percent of all those millions of volunteers work in "human services," a broad category that includes aiding the homeless, family counseling and helping at crisis agencies. Fewer than 4 percent of volunteers work as tutors; and just over 1 percent, as mentors or substance abuse prevention counselors. This is about one-half of those who help in theaters, music and the arts. A separate survey found that roughly 7–15 percent of volunteering done through churches goes outside the walls of the sanctuary into the community.[10] At Tenth Church, for example, its mercy ministries (tutoring, prison, nursing home and homeless) have a volunteer staff of approximately 12 percent of its congregation of fifteen hundred members.

MOTIVATION FOR SERVICE

What motivates people to serve? What do volunteers get out of it? According to Wuthnow's survey, altruism was not high on the list, while self-gratification was. One recurring theme was that volunteering made people feel good about themselves. Deep down, those interviewed expressed selfish reasons for becoming involved—they did it for themselves. One respondent, for instance, said, "I don't feel I have self-worth unless I'm helping people, so I'm really justifying my existence by helping somebody else."[11] A similar sentiment is found in some of my volunteer staff. They feel good about serving others, but not to the degree that their worth is based on it. Their self-worth is based on their relationship with Christ, and the volunteering is done for His glory and honor.

When I asked one prospective volunteer why she wanted to serve in the nursing home, she said, "Deep down everybody has their own selfish reason; they are really doing it for themselves. The same goes for me. It makes me feel good." Then there are those with a different mind-set. One new ministry volunteer committed to helping but then called at the last minute and said that something better had come along. What I read into his comment was the attitude "If being compassionate means I have to sacrifice myself, I'm not going to do it." For this person, the notion that someone will actually want to sacrifice him- or herself for the benefit of others was a distasteful concept. He wanted to put himself first and have his own way.

Those who do serve, volunteer because they want to. They want to do something useful that benefits others and themselves. Or perhaps they volunteer because they feel they should. They have a need for self-esteem and approval, for status and power. Some people say that volunteering makes them "happy." Albert Schweitzer said, "I know not which of you will find happiness, but I do know those of you who find true happiness are those who seek and learn how to serve."[12] Tenth's volunteers serve for a variety of reasons as well. One comment

I hear many times is, "I want to be a blessing to others." But when I ask those who say this about their service, they always tell me how they have been blessed. "It is like God appointed so-and-so to be at my table and say the right word to me," said one volunteer. I remember the time a homeless man with no shoes finished dinner, got up from his table, went to the piano, sat down and played a Beethoven sonata. Everyone was blessed. One person in our homeless ministry started volunteering for selfish reasons. She explains, "It was purely selfish. I moved here in July, two years ago, and I was really lonely. In my neighborhood, there was never anyone around; I felt like I lived in the country and had no neighbors. So I started volunteering." Another volunteer in our homeless outreach stated, "I'm just not a believer in doing something because it's going to get me ahead in the world. I don't care if I am recognized for it. It's just fun to do it." She continues, "If it just happens to benefit me also, then that's like getting two for the price of one; it's a good bargain." In Wuthnow's survey, one Jewish woman shared the following:

> "The Jewish community has been good to us, and we want to repay it." . . . She likes the way people in the community help each other. "All Jews are tied to each other and all of them are obligated to each other. The Hebrew word that is usually translated as charity doesn't mean charity, it means righteousness or justice. . . . The whole notion is to live 'rightly,' because you are called to live that way." . . . She feels that her religion is "the beginning and the end of my life; it's central to how I live."[13]

Volunteering is like any discipline. Each time my volunteers and I serve, we become a little more capable, a little better at helping others. The more we volunteer, the more we see the fullness of people's lives—we no longer see brokenness or suffering; we see real people. The longer we are involved, the more we are able to help them. Our acts of service express goodwill and compassion and bring a certain amount of fulfillment.

We should care for others and find fulfillment by following Christ's example. Those who are in Christ show by their actions who their Master Teacher is. God intends for us to serve others. Serving others is a lifestyle and comes from grateful hearts. The longer we are involved in caring, the more we are able to care for and help others.

Our motivation for service is gratitude and plays an important role as we thank God for our salvation. Gratitude to God should make us hunger and thirst to do right. Grateful for His mercy and grace, we are inspired to help when we see a need. We are grateful that God cares for us, not because He loves us theoretically, but because He has an eternal, loving, caring passion for us. God's concern for us not only indicates His attitude toward us, but also models the attitude that we ought to have toward others, As Christians, we are motivated by God's love, mercy and grace; as good neighbors, we reach out to help others.

HOMELESS OUTREACH VOLUNTEERS

As a follow-up to Wuthnow's survey on volunteerism, I interviewed twelve volunteers who currently work in Tenth

Church's homeless outreach to determine if Christian conviction influences the way people serve. Most said that they act out of gratitude to God and are inspired by books and people who are their role models. They also spoke of a desire to give encouragement and offer hospitality. Another motivating factor was Tenth's actual presence in the city. They also spoke of the need for more volunteers.

GRATITUDE TO GOD

Many agreed that they want to help in any way that is needed. A common sentiment was that because God transformed their lives, they wanted to help others; and because God used someone for their salvation, they wanted to bring saving faith to others.

- One interviewee stated, "The Bible tells us to love God and our neighbors. My involvement is a response to grace. If we are in the Word [of God], how can we not listen to it and consider the needs of others?"

- Another commented, "I minister because God has shared and given so much to me. It would be disrespectful to God not to share with those less fortunate. Jesus plainly states in Matthew 25 [verses 35–36] that ... as we minister to the poor and needy, [we] express ... how much we love God."

- One volunteer coordinator, Vivian, loves the Lord and has a great concern for our homeless neighbors. She combined her love and concern, and for thirty years she has ministered to these neighbors, and she has taught others to do the same.

• Another interviewee, Kevin, was a member of another church that is an hour away from Tenth. He heard of our homeless ministry and decided to check out how we combine evangelism and good works. He fell in love with us and never left. That was twenty-six years ago.

GIVING ENCOURAGEMENT AND OFFERING HOSPITALITY

The interviewees all concluded that encouraging and showing God's love to others is important. "It's hospitality in Jesus' name," one said. Another commented about welcoming our homeless guests, "I need the needy." With one voice, the interviewees said that being with our guests helped lead them to more mature Bible study and prayer life. "We believe that Christians who are more focused in the application of the Word recognize their own weaknesses and how to be aware of others' needs. We've become more compassionate and now see others as Christ sees them."

SHARING THEIR FAITH

Everyone I spoke with enjoys speaking with our guests about Jesus and Scripture.

• "It's part of a lifestyle for us, seeing God at work in relationships. There's hope for now and for all eternity. We like the joy of leading others to Christ and seeing lives transformed."

- About sharing her faith, one person said, "I can make a difference because effective ministry is based on one-on-one relationships. I can tell it makes a difference just by the interaction I have with our guests. And, if I see no results, that does not necessarily mean no difference has been made; it is quite possible that seeds have been sown that will bear fruit at a time to come."

TENTH'S PRESENCE IN THE CITY

Interviewees responded that Tenth is the only church they have attended that cares about the homeless and poor.

- One said, "Tenth wouldn't have these ministries if it didn't care."

- And another, "The ministries here led me from the suburbs to minister in the city. The needs drew me and the pulpit messages led me to pray about doing something. I believe the preaching has planted seeds in my heart. This church chose to stay in the city while other churches left."

MORE PEOPLE COULD BE INVOLVED

A perception of the whole group was that more Christians from Tenth Church should be participating in its outreach ministries. "Very many members don't get involved or give much; this is very disturbing," they said. "We're all called to have real love for our brothers and sisters in Christ, to be concerned for the lost and to be like the Good Samaritan. We must be willing to sacrifice time, energy, convenience, sometimes money and also be willing to enter the pain of others." One individual commented, "Some people have false perceptions about the poor and homeless. They say, 'They are below us—we're not like them!' It's good to reach down and bring someone up. But the Bible says we're all down. . . . We are all needy before God—no one is righteous. Certainly more people could be involved." Someone else said, "It's easy to love people who have homes, etc. It's more difficult to love homeless people when its ninety degrees out, and they're hot and smelly." Another commented, "There's more work and fewer hands. I sometimes get angry, but that is totally unproductive. Instead, I try to repent of the anger and focus on my own repentance and obedience."

Others volunteered for different reasons. One came because he felt guilty not being involved, but then he grew to respect the ministry itself as he matured in his relationship with Christ. Another came reluctantly because a friend wanted her to help. She didn't return for a while, angry with her friend for manipulating her. She stayed away for several months, but then she repented of her selfishness and renewed her involvement. Then there was the volunteer who responded to a pulpit announcement to help at the community dinner. He expected a dinner but did not expect to see homeless people. He didn't understand what he was getting into. While he was annoyed at the "miscommunication," he became ashamed of his un-Christian response. He returned later to regularly volunteer. Every Christian at Tenth Presbyterian Church is a minister and a priest. As priests, we sacrificially heed God's command to love others through the ministry of mercy. Genuinely caring about others requires a personal investment. Tenth Church provides regular mercy ministry training for its members and other Christians in the Philadelphia metropolitan area. We equip and develop servant hearts so these members will serve as good neighbors. By becoming involved with other people and in the problems around us, we learn the language of compassion. Compassion means "to suffer with" another person. In the parable of the good Samaritan, the protagonist of the story "felt for" the condition of the victim. This type of compassion is not visible enough in churches today.

Jesus' teaching presented the world with a model for Christian service. We can only be Christlike in our volunteerism as we deny ourselves, live a cross-life and follow Jesus in serving others. When we do this, we act as the first-century church whose members "were promiscuous with their charity, and the world paid attention."[14] Reconciled to Christ through the cross, the church represents new communities of love and reconciliation; as churches grow in unity of purpose, they call the world to pay attention to us good neighbors.

Questions to Consider

1. What does volunteerism look like at your church?

2. If there is a lack of concern by members to the needs around them, what can you, individually, do to change the status?

3. Who can be your ally in implementing change?

4. When will you begin?

4

LISTENING: HOW TO SHOW THAT WE CARE

L ove listens. If you want to demonstrate your love for others, the first task is to listen. No loving relationship is possible without paying attention by listening. All people, whether young or old, call out to us with expressed needs and desires. The voices may be soft or loud, weak or strong or even silent. They want someone to listen; they want us to understand and feel for them. So, to show love is to listen. Many people feel that no one cares because others "turn a deaf ear" to their sorrow or plea for help.

Here is something I have used in training. It was written by a woman named Jenny who attended a divorce recovery seminar in 1987. I was her small-group facilitator. These are questions Jenny would have asked.

> I hurt and I feel there is no one who cares. No one
> I can talk to—no one who will listen—no one who
> will come alongside, bear my burden and help me
> carry it. I feel lonely ... fearful ... sad. I feel tired and

unwanted. I know there's something better—I'm about to give up. You … will you help me? Could you come alongside me? But, can I trust you? Will you be condescending and humiliate me. Oh, I so need your help. Can you show me respect? Can you understand me without belittling me? Guide me without judging? Listen without dictating? Can you offer me hope? Can you live out God's love to me? Can you show that you care?

FAILING TO KEEP IT TOGETHER

Jenny was a woman who was trying to hold it all together—and failing to do so. She was struggling in every area of her life and felt so miserable, so empty. She tried not to allow the hollowness inside to get the best of her, but it gnawed at her nevertheless. So she kept busy. She had a home, a car and a job. She made do with the clothes she had and would not spend money on whatever was the latest in home entertainment. None of it would fill the void she felt. She was lonely.

Her divorce was somewhat friendly, and it was what she wanted, yet she felt like a failure. Even though a therapist told her such feelings were normal, it didn't help. In today's society, she was told, "You would be abnormal if you didn't have at least one divorce." The experience gave her a new meaning for the word "broken." She felt so frustrated. What she wouldn't give for a raise to ease some of the financial stress.

She was also stressed about her children. Raising them alone was not easy. There were street gangs, drug use near the schools and sexual temptations everywhere. "Don't I have enough to worry about," she thought. She also wondered whether, knowing what she knew now, she would have married and had children. Driving from home, Jenny passes many sacred places—buildings with a cross on top of them. She does not see these churches as a resource. It's been years since she has been inside a church. For her, Sunday is for relaxing or finishing the laundry. Besides, except for one colleague at work, nobody she knows attends church anymore. And who wants to hear sermons on sin, or to sing irrelevant hymns, when what she really needs is help paying the rent, keeping her kids healthy and repairing her low self-image?

According to Jenny and others like her, Christianity hasn't shown itself to be worth considering. Her thought is that the church and its people are not credible or of any help to her.

HELPING JENNY

How should we show Jenny we care? She is divorced, a custodial single parent and lacks much support. Perhaps the one Christian she works with is a member of your church. Although Jenny may not acknowledge that your church exists and could be a possible help to her, your member can be "the church" to her. Because she knows Jenny and her needs, she can alert her church deacons.

If your church member obtained Jenny's permission to speak with a deacon about possible help, that could lead to interest by the deacon in assisting her and arranging to meet with her. The deacon can then set a proper foundation by speaking with Jenny on the phone and establishing the beginnings of trust.

Their appointment takes place at a diner, a neutral location. As you "listen in" on their dialogue, note the indications of difficulty, grief, trauma, hardship, etc. that you see in Jenny's comments. Then see how the deacon (Abe) responds.[1]

> Abe: Thanks for finding the time to meet with me. I guess you don't often get out.
>
> Jenny: I really can't afford it. Sometimes I go out with the kids on their birthdays.
>
> Abe: Do you get a chance to go out with your parents and your family?
>
> Jenny: Not really, we don't talk much since the divorce. They were pretty against it, you know. I go to family get-togethers. But I always feel like I'm the black sheep.
>
> Abe: It sounds like you feel abandoned.
>
> Jenny: Sometimes. But I can't let it bother me. I'm too busy. By the time I get home from school, make supper, do a load of laundry, clean up, help the kids with papers, do homework, drive them to sports … it's hard to find the energy. It's hardest late at night.
>
> Abe: What kind of thoughts come to you then?
>
> Jenny: The kids. I worry about them. We've just

moved for the second time in five years. I needed to do it in order to get away from my former spouse and be close enough to school, but I'm concerned about the effect all of this is having on my children.

Abe: All of the moving is hard on them.

Jenny: Yes it is. They had to change schools in the middle of the year, and they have a hard time making new friends. Stephen is in junior high, and friends are very important to him. He's really angry with me about this.

Abe: How does that leave you feeling?

Jenny: Oh, I just wish I could make everyone happy. But my kids are hurting, and there's not much I can do. Every time I see Stephen feeling upset, I feel worse.

Abe: This situation seems to be really eating at you.

Abe listened well and led the conversation where he wanted it to go. He was a good imitator of such television talk show personalities as Larry King, Oprah Winfrey and Dr. Phil. Notice that he listened and probed for clarification. He asked for more details that would help him understand. His follow-up questions indicated that he paid attention. He showed empathy. He understood and showed respect. Look also at some of Jenny's words, which are highly descriptive of her life and emotions. She said, "I can't afford to eat out," and if she does, it would only be "with the kids on their birthdays." I can hear the pain in her voice. Can you? As a single mom with little income, things are difficult. She indicates that she has a rough relationship with her family since her divorce. Note her statement, "We don't talk much. . . . I feel like the black sheep of the family." She has lost a major support system because of the divorce. When Abe states what he's heard—"it sounds like you feel abandoned"—she covers that up and describes how busy she is, partly so she doesn't have to think about how she really feels. So as not to overwhelm her, Abe was listening and building trust a little at a time.

Let's return to another dialogue that took place at another time.

> Abe: Last time you mentioned that your former spouse is supposed to send monthly child support, but he doesn't always do it. Doesn't that mean your finances are pretty tight sometimes?

> Jenny: It's worse on special days and when school starts. There is just nothing left.

> Abe: I would think that finances create a lot of pressure for you. One thing the church does is pitch in to help. Maybe you could use some help with . . .

> Jenny: (interrupts) I don't know. I don't want anyone to know I'm getting help.

Abe: I can appreciate that. That's why we don't tell anyone. This information is strictly confidential. Only the deacons know.

Jenny: (hesitantly) Oh …

Abe: Does that help?

Jenny: Yes. But I'm still not sure I need the help.

Abe: Why don't we begin by looking at your bills and the list of expenses I asked for when we spoke on the phone. I see that you've brought them.

Jenny: Yes. I have them here.

Abe: As I look at these figures, they show that you just break even. That's a tight squeeze. How do you manage when the car breaks down or when your ex-husband doesn't come through?

Jenny: I don't. (Laughs.) Listen to me here. I am laughing about it. Usually I get upset and start crying. Sometimes I babysit or get a part-time job. I juggle a lot.

Abe: Do you believe you'd benefit from our paying certain bills each month?

Jenny: Yes, but . . .

> Abe: Let me suggest that one of our female financial counselors meets with you. You can work together and agree upon a long-term plan.

> Jenny: I'd like that.

In this conversation, notice that Abe displays the abilities of a good listener. He did not interrupt. He did not respond too soon. He did not jump to any conclusions. He did not try to solve the problems too quickly. He definitely did not take phone calls during the course of the conversation. And he did not judge the speaker.

> Abe: I really appreciate your willingness to share with me. I've learned a lot, and yet I feel like I still have a lot to learn. You need a lot of wisdom and strength in your situation. I am concerned about your finances, but I am praying for you too.

> Jenny: I sure could use prayer.

> Abe: Would you appreciate a time of prayer right now? We've talked about lots of feelings and some struggles. Would you like to share these with God in prayer?

> Jenny: You mean here in the diner?! Well, I guess so.

> Abe: Good. In my prayer I would like to ask God

to keep you close and provide you with wisdom. Is there anything else you'd like us to pray about?

Jenny: How to deal with my son's anger. And I just want some friends to visit with.

Abe: We'll invite God to help you with your son's anger. Let's ask God to lead you to a friend or two. And I'd like to pray that the children would feel at home soon.

Jenny: That would be good.

Abe: Okay let's pray…

KEY INGREDIENTS TO LISTENING

There were some key ingredients to the conversation. The deacon acknowledged the difficulty of the situation. With gentleness and sensitivity, he examined the facts. He asked questions and sought to have Jenny control the conversation. He was open to her thoughts and even thinking outside the box. In fact, he did not bring premanufactured suppositions. He took the meeting as an opportunity to build bridges and to strengthen the relationship. His goal was to achieve a mutually identifiable outcome that would help Jenny in the next stage of her life. The deacon seemed to adhere to these fine points of listening.

1. He listened to understand, not to contradict or refute.

2. He remembered that understanding means paying attention to the tone of voice, the facial expressions and the overall behavior of the speaker.

3. He was careful not to interpret too quickly. He looked for clues to what Jenny was actually trying to say—putting himself in her place (as best he could) and trying to see the world as she saw it—accepting that Jenny's feelings had to be taken into account.

4. He suspended his own opinions for the time being, realizing that he could not listen to himself inwardly and, at the same time, listen outwardly to Jenny.

5. He wasn't impatient. He did not jump ahead of Jenny, but instead gave her time to tell her story.

6. He did not prepare his answer, while he listened. He let Jenny guide the conversation before deciding what to say.

7. He showed interest.

8. He did not interrupt.

9. His purpose wasn't that of a debater. He looked to help Jenny, not to attack her weak spots.

10. Before answering, he summed up what he believed Jenny had said.

In this instance, Abe the deacon, communicated well to Jenny. Good communication represents the idea that the exact sense of the message sent is that which is heard and understood. Abe showed that. Barriers to communication could stem from a lack of interest in what is said or a lack of understanding of the context. Abe definitely showed interest and concern. There are some instances, however, where neither an interest in nor concern for what is being said are present.

AM I COMMUNICATING?

During World War II, the United States government's sale of war bonds was very successful in major cities and their metropolitan areas, but not so much in rural locations. In 1944, a year before the war ended, the *Claude News*, a weekly newspaper published in Texas, wrote a humorous piece imagining how bonds would sell in areas where there were no highways. The article is a tale about communication skills.

> We were told this one about ex-Governor Lehman of New York, who decided that war bonds were not selling too well among the farmers up-state, so Gov. Lehman went himself to help peddle them. After motoring around over dirt roads, he encountered a farmer driving a surrey with no fringe on the top.... "Hi," called out the governor, "did you ever hear of Herbert Lehman of Albany"? "Nope," was the indifferent reply.

The farmer may not have seen many motorcars locally and was probably surprised by the car and that it stopped next to him. Even if Lehman had introduced himself as the governor, the farmer may not have known him. This farmer was literally "out there." That didn't deter the governor who continued:

"Ever hear of Franklin Roosevelt?"

"Nope," said the farmer.

"Pearl Harbor?" continued Lehman.

"Never heard of her either."

"Ever hear of Churchill?"

"Nope, what of it?"

"Well," said Gov. Lehman, "I'm here to see you about bonds."

"Ain't interested," said the farmer as he drove on.

The farmer's wife who was watching through a window greeted her husband with: "Who was that? What did he want?"

"Oh," said the farmer, biting off a chew of tobacco, "some city slicker from Albany—named Lehman— told me about a fellow named Roosevelt—who got into trouble with a girl named Pearl Harbor—from some place near Church Hill—wanted me to go his bond."[2]

To say that the farmer and the governor were worlds apart is an understatement. There were two barriers preventing communication. The farmer didn't know what the governor was saying, and the governor assumed the opposite. So communication involves sending a message in its correct context and knowing that it's intended meaning is received on the other end.

ENTERING A PERSON'S LIFE

What is listening again? Listening is entering into a person's life—coming alongside others while paying close attention to both words and body language. It is being available—showing up, establishing relationships and trusting God for the outcome. Listening is caring. Listeners establish relationships. We show up, trust God for the ministry timetable, offer hope and don't seek to be rescuers. Listeners come alongside and show with both words and body language that they care. Listeners get to know people by "unwrapping their grave-clothes"—peeling off layers of grief and sorrow. Listeners make a difference by providing a biblical alternative to what the world provides. They see a need and attend to it, while others do not. They follow Matthew 25—I was in jail, sick, thirsty, etc. and you ministered to me.

At the beginning of this chapter, I shared the painful words of a woman who attended a divorce recovery seminar. I was her small-group facilitator. She wondered if anyone cared. Could she trust us facilitators or any of the other seminar leaders?

After the seminar, she sent us the following note.

> You saw my loneliness. You cared enough about me to help me in my emptiness. You took the initiative in reaching out to me. You saw my creation in God's image and accepted even the ugly parts of my attitudes and behavior. You listened so you could understand me. You embraced my cold, dark, swirling confusion. You broke through to me in your love, I sampled God's love and I knew I could trust you. Thank you.
>
> You demonstrated to me that we can experience life only to the extent that we experience God. You introduced me to your heavenly Father, our living friend who never leaves, never fails—who is love. At last I'm standing, moving, walking and living in him. You taught me that Christ came to earth that I might have life and have it to the full. You listened and life is not so hard anymore.

As a kid I loved playing baseball. Even though I limped and had difficulty swinging the bat because of partial paralysis in my left hand, a neighbor who was a baseball coach invited me to play organized ball. Although this good neighbor saw my physical condition (which kept me from playing on other teams), he also saw my love for the game and gave me a chance. So I played the game hard and took every opportunity to get my uniform dirty as proof. Similarly, in ministry, we have every opportunity to love hard as good neighbors, by listening and showing compassion. Let us, therefore, reach out to others to make a difference in their lives. As "royal priests," let us be a blessing to others (see 1 Peter 2:9).

Questions to Consider

1. Describe a time when you reached out for help and someone took the time to listen to you. How did you feel?

2. How have you benefited from someone listening to you—
   really listening to you?

3. Describe a time when you reached out for help and someone *didn't* listen to you. How did you feel?

5

HOSPITALITY AS A WAY OF LIFE

Jesus came as one who serves (see Matt. 20:28). He visited and came alongside the broken, the brokenhearted and the lost. He served by giving to others throughout His life and by giving to others in His death. Because the church is called to follow Christ, we must act in the same way. Many who have experienced brokenness have been churched, but they feel rejected by the houses of worship they previously attended because of their own sin or because they have been sinned against. We should give in such a way that those whom we serve with mercy and compassion feel welcomed and are able to worship and know Jesus Christ.

Bobby was one of those who felt rejected because she had HIV disease. I wrote about Bobby in my book *Not Just a Soup Kitchen*. We met Bobby when she felt very much alone and alienated. She didn't feel comfortable in any church—she actually felt hostility toward her. But during her illness, some of our volunteer staff befriended her and invited her to our fellowship. Soon she was studying the Bible with us. And even as her illness gravitated to full-blown AIDS, Bobby became a believer and confessed her faith in Christ. Two years later she died.

Several Tenth members and I attended her memorial service, which was held at an agency for people with AIDS. The memorial offered no hope, had no Bible reading, and the officiating minister never mentioned Bobby's faith in Christ. Following the service, I introduced myself to the agency's director, explained our relationship to Bobby and asked him if we could have a Bible study there. He said he could not make the decision—it was something the staff and clients would have to agree upon together. He arranged a meeting the following week. There were gays, lesbians, intravenous drug users and cross-dressers at the meeting, along with agency staff and several members of Tenth Church. After the agency director introduced the meeting's topic—that we were proposing a Bible study—I explained our relationship with Bobby, how Bobby had become a believer, how she had a new life in Christ and hope in the midst of crisis. I said that our goal for the Bible study was to teach the Scriptures and to establish relationships with those who attended the study.

Suddenly, as if no one heard these words, people began bombarding me with questions.

- One person said, "Will you try to change us?"

- Another asked, "Are you going to try to make us Presbyterian?"

- Next was, "Are you going to forbid homosexuals from attending?"

- And then, "Will transvestites be allowed to attend?"

To these questions I repeated the reasons already stated for the Bible study: We wanted to share the hope and new life that we believe are found in the Bible, and we wanted to develop relationships with those who attend the Bible study. We said that we could not change anyone's behavior—only God has the power to do that. We said we were not teaching any denominational program but only the Word of God found in the Bible. We said that everyone was welcome to attend and that the Bible study would not be a platform for "gay bashing." We referred again and again to our relationship with Bobby and the new hope that she had as a person with AIDS. The response of those we met with, I believe, was voiced in the statement of one person who stood up and said, "What the hell. Why not? We need all the help we can get." And as I looked around the room, everyone seemed to be agreeing. As a result, a weekly Bible study was established. Attacks came and went. And six months later, in addition to the study, they requested a worship service.

THE FRUIT OF HOSPITALITY

What did we learn from that experience? We learned that those we met with had these expectations about churches and Christians. They expected that we would be unfriendly. We treated them with kindness. They expected that we would be unwelcoming. We provided a warm welcome. In fact, we removed the "strangerness." They expected to be labeled and stigmatized. In our kindness, we removed the stigma. Most of all, they expected hostility. We extended hospitality. What did we do exactly? Quite simply, we made ourselves available. We became involved. We established relationships. And we offered hope. In other words, we showed them hospitality.

What is hospitality? From basic observation, here are my definitions:

1. HOSPITALITY is the business of providing catering, lodging and entertainment service.

2. HOSPITALITY is the cordial or friendly reception and kindness of welcoming guests or strangers.

3. HOSPITALITY is a key ingredient of family life—the ability to welcome people of diverse backgrounds with an offering of food and shelter.

4. HOSPITALITY is the practice of being hospitable.

5. Then there is my own favorite definition:
   HOSPITALITY is the opposite of hostility.

Let's focus on the lifestyle and attitude of what it means for Christians to be hospitable. If we go back to the definitions, we see the phrase "welcoming guests or strangers." That is essentially what we do when we offer hospitality: We invite people into our homes or churches or lives in such a way that they feel welcome. The act of hospitality turns strangers into guests. It removes stigmatizing labels and creates a safe place for people to come. It integrates the Great Commission into our lives.

We see this in the way Abraham responded in Genesis 18 when he welcomes three guests out of the hot sun and into his tents. The morning chores were complete, and workers had returned to their tents for the customary siesta. The sheep, donkeys and camels were clumped under the shade of the trees. And Abraham was sitting at the shaded entrance of his own tent enjoying a rest. Perhaps he had nodded off because all of a sudden he saw three men standing nearby. Abraham had neither seen them nor heard them approach. They were simply there.

> The LORD appeared to him by the oaks of Mamre, as he sat at the door of his tent in the heat of the day. He lifted up his eyes and looked, and behold, three men were standing in front of him. When he saw them, he ran from the tent door to meet them and bowed himself to the earth and said, "O Lord, if I have found favor in your sight, do not pass by your servant. Let a little water be brought, and wash your feet, and rest yourselves under the tree, while I bring a morsel of bread, that you may refresh yourselves, and after that you may pass on— since you have come to your servant." So they said, "Do as you have said." (18:1–5)

The ministry of hospitality also focuses on people's needs: their physical and spiritual needs, their heartache, their need for refuge, nourishment, a listening ear and acceptance. Hospitality can happen in a messy home or a neat one, around a dinner table or on a park bench. The main dish can be a can of soup or a sandwich or just the sharing of ourselves and the love of Christ. But when we see a need, we should respond as we are able. Abraham shows us how.

> And Abraham went quickly into the tent to Sarah and said, "Quick! Three seahs of fine flour! Knead it, and make cakes." And Abraham ran to the herd and took a calf, tender and good, and gave it to a young man, who prepared it quickly. Then he took curds and milk and the calf that he had prepared, and set it before them. (Gen. 18:6–8)

A little water? A morsel of bread? A little snack? No!! Freshly killed and cooked veal, fresh baked bread and cheese. A feast! Verse 8 continues, "And he stood by them under the tree while they ate." Consider the enormity of this feast. A young calf weighs around seventy-five pounds. This is not a piece of meat that can be prepared quickly. And what about the bread or cake? Abraham tells Sarah to take twenty-one quarts (i.e., twenty-three pounds) of flour. That is enough for a heavenly host! Not to mention all the cheese "curds" and milk.

What do we see here? A maître d' seeing to every need of someone with a regular reservation. Or a waiter zealously attending to his favorite dinner guests. You would want a deacon like that!

Here Abraham served the Lord personally. And this is our biblical example. Abraham was ninety-nine years old and wealthy. He could have entrusted this task to his chief steward or one of his more than three hundred servants (see Gen. 14:14). Instead, he decided to minister to the Lord personally. He also ministered immediately. Abraham could have ignored them by pretending to be asleep, or he could have asked them to sit down and wait until he had finished his rest. But Abraham was a man of faith, and a faithful servant does not delay when it comes to serving others. Abraham ministered to the Lord speedily. Genesis 18:2 says "he ran" to meet the visitors. Verse 6 says he "went quickly" to tell Sarah to bake some bread. Then he ran to get a tender calf and saw to it that a servant quickly prepared and cooked the meat (see 18:7). This is an old man running around in the heat of the day! Only after he had served his guests did this deacon stand still (see 18:8). The following words of Scripture were not yet written, yet Abraham exemplified them fully: "Do not withhold good from those to whom it is due, when it is in your power to do it" (Prov. 3:27); and "As we have opportunity, let us do good to everyone" (Gal. 6:10).

HOW DO WE PUT HOSPITALITY INTO PRACTICE TODAY?

In 1984, Tenth Church started providing hospitality to those who are homeless, poor, lonely, alienated, abused and brokenhearted. It began with a "Thanksgiving Community Dinner" when our deacons invited our neighbors to attend. Since then, we have held a community dinner every month. What do we do? We worship together; then we sit, eat and talk. But we are not a soup kitchen. We are a Christian alternative. Soup kitchens, in general, are impersonal. People come in, pick up a plate, receive ladles of food, sit down, eat and leave. There may be brief conversation. But, most often, not.

We are different. The community dinner ministry is a monthly banquet. It is personal, it is one-on-one and it is evangelistic. Here's how it works: Imagine you are in the sanctuary of Tenth Presbyterian Church. It is the second Sunday of the month. The time is 1:00 p.m. Your eyes are closed; but you hear songs of praise, a solo or two, a testimony and a gospel message. You open your eyes and see one hundred people singing, praying, shouting for joy and attentive to the gospel message. At 2:15 p.m. you climb the stairs to Fellowship Hall. You see the worshipers sitting at tables with church members. Your eyes also catch sight of twenty teens from a partnering church who will serve the food. And, through a window, you see more people preparing food in the kitchen.

There is a hum of conversation at the tables; you see lots of smiles and friendly greetings and you think: *This is great!* Then you hear the buzz of the microphone and me saying, "Hi. I'm glad you're all here. For the next hour and a half, I want you to relax and enjoy yourselves. The format for the community dinner is restaurant-style. You don't have to get up except to use the restrooms. Servers will be bringing both the food and the drinks. You don't need to get up for anything because you are our guests."

I give thanks for the food, and the meal is served. You lean against the wall, and a kitchen volunteer tells you, "The food, itself, is a ministry, you know. We put lots and lots of love into what is served, how nutritious it is and even how it looks." You glance around the room. She is right. The taste, the aroma, how it appears on the plate is ministering to everyone. She then points out that the teenaged servers are sweating already but notes that they are smiling too. You see that they're having fun and are learning a lot about how Christ calls us to serve. As you walk around Fellowship Hall, you see each table host is engaged in conversation. After dinner, as the guests are leaving, you see lots of smiles and hugs and hear some of our staff arrange to meet guests afterward for fellowship and Bible study. By doing this consistently, we reinforce our call to be good neighbors.

THOSE WHOM GOD CALLS

Who are the staff? They are members who reside in each of Tenth's geographic parishes along with other churches who partner with us. Each month, one parish sponsors the dinner and sends members to serve with us. These members are young, old, single, married, black, white, Asian and Latino. They help set up, cook and serve as table hosts. And for the wait staff, each month one of our partnering churches provides teens and young adults. We also have other volunteers who have committed to help regularly. Among them are two volunteers I want to mention: Peter and Bill.

TEN-YEAR-OLD PETER

Peter was ten years old when I met him. God had put on his heart a concern for homeless men and women. And so one day he showed up at the community dinner. Confidently, he looked me in the eye and said, "I want to be a dinner host. I want to sit at a table with our homeless guests." I have to say that this brought a huge smile to my face and joy to my heart. Here was a preadolescent with a servant's heart. If he asked you whether or not he, as a young boy, could sit at a table with strangers, what would you say? If you knew that some of his table guests were drug addicts, ex-offenders, someone with HIV disease or mental illness, what would your advice to him be? I considered all this. I desired so much that he sit at a table with our guests. He had no fear and had so much of Christ's love to offer. So I showed gratitude and encouragement. I then offered several options.

First of all, I told him how much I appreciated his desire to help. I thanked him for the Christlike attitude he showed in wanting to offer hospitality to those who receive little kindness and love. I encouraged him to speak with his parents before I made any decision, and I encouraged him to come back and tell me what they said. Peter did speak with his parents, who told him that they really could not approve of him hosting a table. They suggested that, as a family, they speak with me together. Peter, with his parents, approached me, and the mom and dad expressed their concern about their ten-year-old son hosting a table. You should have seen the expression on the face of this young servant. I have heard other parents describe this as a "boo-boo" face. How disappointed he looked!

I told the parents that I supported their decision but asked that they consider sitting at a table with their son. This way they would be able to participate and monitor what occurred at the table. Peter turned to them with a "Please mom, please dad, can I . . . can I . . . huh?" look in his eyes. They answered that they would not feel comfortable doing that. Peter, once again, looked glum and dejected. I wanted to make it possible for Peter to serve in some way, even though his role would not be to host the table. So I told him that there were many opportunities to participate in the dinner, and every opportunity was important. Some people assist in the worship service. Others purchase and cook the food. Many more serve the food to our guests. And there are those who set up the tables, chairs, table covers, utensils, decorations and *Daily Bread* booklets. I assured Peter that we could not do without one or the other and that if he and his parents worked together to provide one of these services, its value would be great. He again looked at his parents and asked, "Can we help set up?" When they said that they could, he smiled. For two years this whole family served with us—a young boy with the heart of a servant and his parents, who he led on a wonderful journey of good neighboring. When they moved out of state, I heard that Peter and his family were once again serving together.

EIGHTY-ONE-YEAR-OLD BILL

Bill was another very unique volunteer. I first met him when he was eighty-one years old, and Jesus had just changed his life. Bill had been a nominal Christian for many years—until a heart attack that resulted in the implant of a necessary pacemaker. Bill decided at that point to completely surrender his life to Jesus and to serve Him. He chose to serve with the community dinner to share his faith with our homeless and poor neighbors. Because he had been a radio announcer, Bill enjoyed using his crisp, clear voice to welcome our guests, give his testimony and tell stories of God's faithfulness. He enjoyed hosting a table with seven dinner guests, sharing the good news of Jesus Christ and getting to know our homeless neighbors. He also led a prison Bible study until his death at age ninety-three. Though he used public transportation (usually a seventy-five-minute trip), neither rain, nor sleet, nor snow, nor stormy weather, nor arthritis would keep Bill from his appointed duty. (Only a hip replacement and the insertion of a new heart pacemaker kept him away.) Jesus gave him a servant's heart and a commitment as a good neighbor to serve others.

HOSPITALITY'S EFFECTS ON ME

My life was changed by Jesus through this ministry. At my first community dinner in 1988, I met a man named Horace. I never saw him again. I have no idea whether he was an angel sent to test me or not. We sat next to each other, so I introduced myself and started a conversation. I thought this would be an easy task. Over my many years in social work I had spoken to many people of various backgrounds and felt comfortable doing so. I began by saying, "Who are your heroes?" I figured that Horace and I and the six others at our table would talk about something we could all relate to, like a sports or political leader or a figure in social justice. So when I said, "Who are your heroes?" he looked me right in the eye and remained silent for a moment. It was an awkward moment for me. Then he said, "What do you mean heroes? Just look around this room!" (There were about 120 homeless guests seated at tables.) "Look at them. They are all losers, including myself. Every one of us," he said, "is a no-good rotten bastard." At that point I felt very small, inadequate and embarrassed. I didn't know what to say next. My inclination was to sink under the table or disappear entirely. As I recall, I changed the subject and began talking about football—"How about those Eagles?" Looking back in reflection, I learned a lot from the experience: Horace's description of our unsaved condition was so accurate. But when we come to salvation in Christ, we are no longer losers, or no-good, or rotten or illegitimate. We are no longer bastards. In Christ, we become worthy, adopted children of God the Father. Though our "sins are like scarlet" (Isa. 1:18) and "our righteous acts are like filthy rags" (64:6, NIV), in Christ's righteousness we are heirs, children of our victorious, almighty God.

That hosting experience always encourages me to use the illustration about children who are unwanted, unloved and abandoned and our hospitable, heavenly Father who wants to come alongside them, love them and adopt them. From 1997 to 2000, my wife and I did foster care. We took in a two-year-old girl who had been abandoned in a park by her drug-addicted mother. She had been left in the custody of her eight-year-old sister, also abandoned. When found, the girls were filthy, and bugs were crawling on the two-year-old. She was cleaned up on the outside when we took her into our home. The first night, when her eyes became heavy, she took a newspaper and laid it on the stairs. She then set herself on top of the newspaper to sleep.

She was unclean when she was found. But we neighbored her. We showed her our love and the love of many church members—and we would have adopted her. But after time in prison and rehab, the birth mother worked hard and was reunited with her daughters.

When we practice hospitality, we come alongside others. We become involved. We establish relationships with those who have lost their support system and with those who are grieving or brokenhearted. I opened this chapter with the story of Bobby and how the people we met with after her death had certain expectations. These members of the LGBT community had expected us to be hostile. They expected us to reject them. They expected us to be uncivil and less than kind. Because we had servant hearts, we were able to show them the true love and hospitality of Jesus. We were able to bring to Him more who felt alienated from God. We did all of this because we sought out those who were despised and friendless. We welcomed the stranger. We were good neighbors in the name of Jesus.

I am reminded of Matthew 25:34-40 when Jesus speaks about the final judgment.

> The King will say to those on his right, "Come, you who are blessed by my Father, inherit the kingdom prepared for you from the foundation of the world. For I was hungry and you gave me food, I was thirsty and you gave me drink, I was a stranger and you welcomed me, I was naked and you clothed me, I was sick and you visited me, I was in prison and you came to me." Then the righteous will answer him, saying, "Lord, when did we see you hungry and feed you, or thirsty and give you drink? And when did we see you a stranger and welcome

you, or naked and clothe you? And when did we see you sick or in prison and visit you?" And the King will answer them, "Truly, I say to you, as you did it to one of the least of these my brothers, you did it to me."

Did you ever notice that when Jesus mentions how people will inherit His kingdom, he doesn't mention a Christian's theology, eschatology, or soteriology; how they vote; how many people they share the gospel with; or how much money they contribute to the church? He doesn't mention any of these. What He does mention, however, is people's being good neighbors—whether they provided food and clothing to the poor, quenched their thirst, and visited the sick and the prisoner. If you were a neighbor to them, He says, you were a neighbor to Him.

Questions to Consider

1. What does hospitality look like at your church?

2. Are people well represented? If not, who is missing?

3. What is your ministry passion? To what local people or group do you want to serve?

4. How can you help your church expand its outreach to include these?

6

THE CHURCH AT WORK

Someone once asked Jesus the question, "What must we do to do the works God requires?" To that He answered, "The work of God is this: to believe in the one he has sent" (John 6:28–29, NIV). It is in this work that we can perform good works.

In concert, the *Westminster Confession of Faith* states:

> These good works, done in obedience to God's commandments, are the fruits and evidences of a true and lively faith: and by them believers manifest their thankfulness, strengthen their assurance, edify their brethren, adorn the profession of the Gospel, stop the mouths of the adversaries, and glorify God, whose workmanship they are, created in Christ Jesus thereunto, that, having their fruit unto holiness, they may have the end, eternal life.[1]

In his commentary on Philippians (see Phil. 2:12–13), James M. Boice states, "We are to act in light and wonder of 'so great a salvation.' Good doctrine always leads to practical Christianity. Because God has already entered your life, you have his power at work within you. As God works in you, work out your salvation by expressing it in action." [2] As followers of Jesus, we don't just proclaim the message of the gospel. We live it out as citizens of the kingdom of God. We proclaim the gospel message in both word and deed. For example, we declare in our mercy ministry: "There is no mercy without the gospel (the good news of Jesus Christ)." We gather together with those in prison, in nursing homes or living on the street, worshiping, singing, studying the Bible or sharing a meal together.

We are all helpers contributing to the church household. In this, we show how God has given us gifts "for the common good" (1 Cor. 12:7), and all gifts are needed. None of us is unnecessary or useless. We may even help so often that we might not be aware of it. Listening to someone's struggles, commiserating with an anxious friend, giving godly advice to a small-group member, asking how we can pray. We were meant to live that way. According to Christian counselor Ed Welch:

> We were meant to walk side by side, an interdependent body of weak people. God is pleased to grow and change us through the help of people who have been re-created in Christ. . . . Friends are the best helpers. They come prepackaged with compassion and love. . . . We ordinary people have been given power and wisdom through the Holy Spirit

and are called to love others (John 13:34). From this beginning, we are compelled to move toward others rather than stay away. . . . You are one of the ordinary people God uses to help others. . . . Jesus will be in it and over it. . . . He also came to serve rather than to be served, and he did it side by side. As far as we are able, we do this with one another.[3]

If we all looked after the people in our circle of friends, then everyone would be cared for. We could also work through a particular Bible study (by topic or book of the Bible) with others at lunchtime, during the day or after work. This would create new ministry opportunities and be thirty minutes of very effective ministry.

WE ARE SENT

Several years ago, Tenth Church's Urban Missions Conference brochure said, "We are a sent people witnessing to salvation in Christ and participating to build up the church. Our mission (a) begins in worship, (b) ministers in evangelism and compassion, (c) encourages believers toward Christian maturity through discipleship, and (d) prepares women, men, teens and children for service." Our mission as believers includes reaching out to others. And by reaching out, more and more of our neighbors and colleagues will find their way to Christ (and your church).

We are always preparing for this mission of demonstrating biblical love to others—not as an "evangelism program," but as a natural display of Christ's love to others. Because we have relationships with unbelieving neighbors and those in and near our workplaces, we can easily invite them to home or work Bible studies and worship. And we should seek after our neighbor's eternal good and be involved in friendly evangelism and blessing them in spiritual ways.

The Scripture passages commonly known as the Beatitudes speak about our spiritual blessings in Christ (see Matt. 5:1–12; Luke 6:20–23): Blessed are the poor in spirit, blessed are those who mourn, blessed are the meek, blessed are those who hunger and thirst for righteousness, blessed are the merciful, blessed are the pure in heart, blessed are the peacemakers, and blessed are those who are persecuted for righteousness. Here Jesus describes the riches that belong to those who are His. The Beatitudes demonstrate that heavenly blessedness is the opposite of worldly desire for monetary wealth, merriment, abundance, etc. The Beatitudes describe our riches in Christ and what is possible to unbelievers too.

But there are not only beatitudes, there are also "hospitalitudes." Here is how Pat Ennis describes them in her book *Practicing Hospitality.*

- [Blessed] are those who practice biblical hospitality.

- [Blessed] are those who "pursue the love of strangers."

- [Blessed] are those who include people of all cultures on their guest lists.

- [Blessed] are those who develop hospitality management skills.

- [Blessed] are those who intentionally extend hospitality to "the others"—singles, widows, the grieving . . . and those experiencing food insecurity.

- [Blessed] are those whose homes are both a place of refuge and a center for evangelism.

- [Blessed] are those who do not become disillusioned in practicing biblical hospitality.

- [Blessed] are those who acknowledge that they are unable to practice biblical hospitality in their own strength, for by this means they learn that the Lord's power overcomes their weaknesses and allows them to become vessels used for his honor and glory.[4]

This type of mind-set and this kind of neighboring should be in our DNA. The "hospitalitudes" are merely a way of putting the joy of hospitality into action. They are the user-friendly way of showing daily that we have servant hearts. And every day is a day for hospitality. Sunday especially is a day to exercise this gift. According to former Tenth Church pastor James Boice, "We are not justified by works. If we are trying to be justified by works, we are not Christians. But neither can we claim to be Christians if we do not have works" (see Matt. 25:14-30). "Surely, we are missing the boat if Sunday is not a day of spiritual refreshment [and] evangelistic opportunity"[5] (see Rom. 14:5-6). As neighbors, let us welcome the lonely, encourage those who are down, befriend the friendless and visit the sick. And let us show the world that we, the people of God, have servant hearts.

Questions to Consider

1. How has God prepared you for good works?

2. Where are you serving Him?

3. What are the needs of that ministry?

4. How can you encourage others to participate?

7

VISITATION

The word "visit" has many connotations in today's world. One of its uses in the Bible is found in James 1:27: "Religion that is pure and undefiled before God the Father is this: to visit orphans and widows in their affliction, and to keep oneself unstained from the world."

Today, my understanding of that visitation includes not only widows and orphans, but also those who have been abused or have lost their support systems. It includes those who are in need, the sick, the friendless and any who may be in distress. Thus, visitation includes coming alongside, providing a listening ear and shepherding.

Our "visiting" of orphans and widows (and others who have lost their support) in their distress involves a ministry that imparts life and hope and provides restoration. Our ministry must also help connect them to Jesus—to allow them, at last or once again, to bear fruit.[1] This is seen in Tenth's outreach ministry.

VISITING LARRY

Larry isolated himself so much that no one knew his problems, and no one visited with him. This Tenth Church neighbor was addicted to alcohol and other drugs for eighteen years. If you saw him, you would have said he looked like a "walking dead man." Larry had an interesting "abode." He put his pillow on the steps of the synagogue located one block from Tenth and slept there. He was frequently seen by church members who lived in the area or walked by. Many would stop and speak with Larry as he was a gentle soul and presented no threat to anyone. He even walked the dogs of some nearby residents.

One member's interest in Larry grew over the years. Early on, Betsy actually avoided Larry. She was fearful of him and either crossed the street or intentionally walked on the other side, looking away when she passed by. She also ignored him when he walked past her. Months later, she began greeting him. Soon they discovered each other's names. And finally, she brought Larry a sandwich and sat with him on the synagogue steps while he ate.

While sitting next to him regularly, Betsy learned some things about him. He was "churched" as a kid but wandered away. One of his street names was "Moses" because he had memorized many Old Testament stories. Betsy shared her faith as she visited with him, showing him the love of Christ and inviting him to Tenth's Fellowship Bible Study, where we welcome many of our homeless neighbors. Larry resisted and stayed away. This did not deter Betsy. She continued to speak with him and invite him to Tenth, and he finally accepted the invitation. One cold winter's day, he showed up for a hot meal in a warm room. He expected that much, but he did not expect to receive a warm welcome and Christian hospitality.

This was the beginning of my friendship with Larry. Several years later, he became a Christian, overcame his drug addiction and became a member of Tenth Church. He was then reunited with the mother of his children, and they wed. All of them came to saving faith in our Lord Jesus Christ. He and his wife became employed, and they purchased a home. Today he is ministering to people who are still in their addiction to drugs.

I remember the turning point for Larry's new faith journey. One day he came to see me at Tenth. It was a typical August summer—very hot, hazy and humid. He had slept on the street the night before; and when he came in to see me, he was filthy, he smelled terrible and he was crying. "I am sick and tired of being sick and tired," he said. He also told me that he was ready to surrender his life and let Jesus help him. He had seen Jesus' love through the care of Christians at Tenth. He witnessed a model of service that was new to him—a church that showed it cared about those who are afflicted.

Visitation involves bringing life and hope. Its biblical context is coming alongside those in despair, sharing our lives with others and inviting them to know the richest of life.

GIVING LIFE

A biblical example is found in First Samuel 1. We read that a godly Old Testament woman could not have children and, because of that, was treated harshly by others. When God "visited" Hannah—the word connoted the giving of life. She prayed to God: "O LORD of hosts, if you will indeed look on the affliction of your servant and remember me and not forget your servant, but will give to your servant a son, then I will give him to the LORD all the days of his life, and no razor shall touch his head" (1 Sam. 1:11). The result was that God "visited" Hannah and, over the years, gave her five children. First Samuel 2:21 says, "The LORD visited Hannah, and she conceived and bore three sons and two daughters. And the boy Samuel grew in the presence of the LORD."

God answered Hannah's prayer with Samuel and, in turn, she honored her pledge to "give him to the Lord all the days of his life." God saw her suffering. He visited her, and Hannah conceived. God's visitation brought life.

Another example where God visited and gave life is found in Luke 7:11–16. Here Jesus has entered a town just as a funeral procession is taking place. A young man who died is mourned by his mother, a widow. Jesus sees her and is moved with compassion. He turns to the mother and says, "Do not weep." He then touches the coffin and says, "Young man, I say to you, arise." The passage continues, "And the dead man sat up and began to speak, and Jesus gave him to his mother. Fear seized them all, and they glorified God, saying, 'A great prophet has arisen among us!' and 'God has visited his people!'" Everyone who witnessed this knew God had visited them because he brought life to the dead. When we visit, we bring fullness to places that are empty. Where there is darkness, our visit brings light. Where there is fruitlessness and sorrow, our ministry points others to Jesus and the fruit that only He can provide. Jesus is the giver of life and hope to all who are in need. In addition to giving life, the word "visit" in Scripture is connected with the idea of rescue and redemption. Exodus 3:16–17 says that God visited His people. God tells Moses to gather the elders together and say to them "The LORD, the God of your fathers, the God of Abraham, of Isaac, and of Jacob, has appeared to me." Tell them, "I [the Lord] have observed you and what has been done to you in Egypt, and I promise that I will bring you up out of the affliction of Egypt to the land . . . flowing with milk and honey." Here is a connection between God's visiting the Israelites and His plans to deliver them from slavery. Here, His visit involves rescue and deliverance.

Similarly, in Luke 1:68, Zechariah foretells the coming of the Deliverer. Previously unable to have children, his wife Elizabeth gives birth to a son, John, who will be Jesus' forerunner. He says, "Blessed be the Lord God of Israel, for he has visited and redeemed his people." Zechariah continues, speaking now about his son:

> And you, child, will be called the prophet of the Most High; for you will go before the Lord to prepare his ways, to give knowledge of salvation to his people in the forgiveness of their sins, because of the tender mercy of our God, whereby the sunrise shall visit us from on high to give light to those who sit in darkness and in the shadow of death, to guide our feet into the way of peace. (Luke 1:76–79)

God made Zechariah and Elizabeth fruitful and useful for the proclamation of the Messiah's visitation.

God came to visit us in human form. Jesus came and dwelt with us (see John 1:14). He shined on people living in darkness and in the shadow of death, to rescue and redeem them (and us) from the clutches of sin and death (see Matt. 4:16). And now we, the body of Christ, are called to visit those who live in darkness and in the shadow of death. We are to bring the light of Christ to those to whom Jesus reveals His heart of compassion.

OFFERING HOPE

To whom did Christ show compassion? He touched and healed those with disabilities, diseases and illness.

> "He went throughout all Galilee, teaching in their synagogues and proclaiming the gospel of the kingdom and healing every disease and every affliction among the people. . . . And they brought him all the sick, those afflicted with various diseases and pains, those oppressed by demons, those having seizures, and paralytics, and he healed them" (Matt. 4:23–24).

> Jesus saw a woman who was permanently bent over, had compassion for her and said, "Woman, you are freed from your disability" (Luke 13:12).

> At Bethesda, "lay a multitude of invalids—blind, lame and paralyzed. One man was there who had been an invalid for thirty-eight years. When Jesus

saw him lying there and knew that he had already been there a long time, he said to him, 'Do you want to be healed?' The sick man answered him, 'Sir, I have no one to put me into the pool when the water is stirred up, and while I am going, another steps down before me.' Jesus said to him, 'Get up, take up your bed, and walk'" (John 5:2–8).

"In that hour he healed many people of diseases and plagues and evil spirits, and on many who were blind he bestowed sight" (Luke 7:21).

Some people were healed because of their faith.

"A woman who had suffered from a discharge of blood for twelve years came up behind him and touched the fringe of his garment, for she said to herself, 'If I only touch his garment, I will be made well.' Jesus turned, and seeing her he said, 'Take heart, daughter; your faith has made you well.' And instantly the woman was made well" (Matt. 9:20–22).

"A leper came to him, imploring him, and kneeling said to him, 'If you will, you can make me clean.' Moved with pity, he stretched out his hand and touched him and said to him, 'I will; be clean'" (Mark 1:40–41).

God also provides for those who have emotional problems.

> "The LORD builds up Jerusalem; he gathers the outcasts of Israel. He heals the brokenhearted and binds up their wounds" (Ps. 147:2–3).

And He raises the dead.

> "Then Jesus, deeply moved again, came to the tomb. It was a cave, and a stone lay against it. . . . He cried out with a loud voice, 'Lazarus, come out.'" (John 11:38, 43).

Visitation is a biblical and exciting ministry of bringing the light and life of Christ to those who live in darkness. We make a difference by visiting. When "the Word became flesh and dwelt among us," (1:14), He tabernacled with us—He "pitched His tent" next door and got to know all about us. Jesus, the Good Shepherd, rescued each of us. So, in a unique way, we are called to be shepherds, following His example. Jesus works through us as we follow His example and "visit" others. He is our model for service. He healed, encouraged, comforted and strengthened those in His path. He shed tears, and He died in order to save us. Jesus is our model for being a good neighbor, for having a servant's heart, for listening, for providing hospitality and much more.

Questions to Consider

1. What did you learn anew about visitation?

2. Where are you bringing hope and new light?

3. How can you share this at your church?

4. Who will help you?

8

SHEPHERDING

Jesus, we are told in John 10:11, is the Good Shepherd who visits and cares for His sheep. And we are in need of that shepherd, as we are "like sheep without a shepherd" (Mark 6:34). Sheep and people have similar characteristics. Both sheep and people are often fearful and timid. They are often stubborn and stupid. They are always getting into trouble. Nevertheless, Jesus provides for His sheep. He is the Good Shepherd.

Psalm 23 indicates just how Jesus provides for us as if we were sheep. The psalmist says, "The Lord is my shepherd," plus "I shall not want" and "He makes me lie down." What do sheep want and need? They will not lie down and rest easy until they are free of all fear and irritation. There is usually conflict with other sheep (thus the term "butting heads"). They are rarely free from pests. And they cannot find the right food by themselves.

Similarly, we are settled until we feel discomforted by life's hazards (fear). We are discontent with our relationships (friction). We lack confidence and calmness in the face of frustrations and futility (pests). We need to be drawn near to God to truly feast on His Word.

SHEPHERDING

What does the shepherd do? He provides for his sheep, rescues them from danger, heals their afflictions and diseases. What does the "Good Shepherd" do? Jesus saves us, restores us and provides for us. The Gospels and Psalms give several illustrations. Psalm 42:11 reads, "Why are you cast down, oh my soul?" A cast sheep is one that has turned over on its back and cannot get up by itself. If it is not rescued soon enough, the sheep will die from emanating gases. If a shepherd is missing a wandering sheep, the first thought is that it might be "cast." There is also danger from predators like dogs, coyotes, cougars and vultures.

We don't use the expression "cast people," but many of us become emotionally or spiritually incapable of helping ourselves—perhaps even have trouble getting out of bed in the morning. Some of us, like the psalmist, are disquieted. We lack hope and are incapable of helping ourselves. Years ago, I suffered a great personal loss. The weightiness of that burden seemed to be more than I could bear, and my daily routine became somewhat self-destructive.

While I got up and went to work each day, I otherwise made myself a prisoner in my apartment. Basically all I did, besides work, was eat, drink liquor, watch TV and sleep. I was afraid to go out—afraid that I would see people who were happy, which made me feel even worse. Thankfully, God sent friends as shepherds to care for me until, after twelve months, I was no longer cast down.

Jesus heals us when we are tortured by difficult situations and difficult people. Just like nasal flies and insects that get under a sheep's wool, people can be tortured by various life situations and by other people who "get under their skin." In addition, we can be self-inflicted by our own negative thoughts, ideas, emotions and choices.

In his book *A Shepherd Looks at Psalm 23*, Phillip Keller describes the many aspects of shepherding, the person of the shepherd and the sheep themselves. These include having no needs, being provided for by a caring individual and being protected from dangers of all kinds. According to Keller, I shall not want is the sense that sheep are totally satisfied with their owner and totally content with their lives. Sheep need green grass, fresh water, shade, safety and shelter from storms. They need relief from wounds, bruises, disease and parasites. It is the shepherd in their lives who makes the difference in the sheep's destiny.[1] Similarly, we have personal struggles, hardships and even calamities.

Yet, because we belong to Christ, we have access to Him as Lord and Savior, along with the peace that passes all understanding. This is the understanding I had after my friends shepherded me during my time of depression described previously. I felt shipwrecked and had to turn to the captain of my soul for rescue.

As followers of the Good Shepherd, we can boast in the Lord that He is our shepherd—we shall not want. We are completely satisfied with His watchfulness of our lives. Why? Because He is the shepherd of His flock and no trouble is too great for Him. He is on the job twenty-four seven to care for His sheep in every detail.

The shepherd is the owner who delights in his flock. For him there is no greater reward, no deeper satisfaction, than that of seeing his sheep contented, well fed, safe and flourishing under his care. This is indeed his very life. He gives his all. He will go to no end of trouble and labor to find them the finest grazing, the richest pasturage, ample winter feed and clean water. He will spare himself no pain to provide shelter from storms, and protection from ruthless enemies and the diseases and parasites to which sheep are so susceptible. No wonder Jesus said, "I am the good shepherd. The good shepherd lays down his life for the sheep" (John 10:11). And again, "I am come that they might have life, and that they might have it more abundantly" (10:10, KJV). [2] The diligent shepherd sees that his sheep are fit, content and able to stand on their feet. He can tell if they were injured during the night, and throughout the day he watches to make sure all is well.

The Good Shepherd makes me lie down. Sheep are unable to lie down unless they are free from fear, free from the pressure of any butting order, free from flies and parasites, and free from hunger. Only the shepherd can provide an escape from fear, tension, aggravation and hunger. "As long as there is even the slightest suspicion of danger from dogs, coyotes, cougars, bears or other enemies, the sheep stand up ready to flee for their lives." [3] Keller says, "I came to realize that nothing so quieted and reassured the sheep as to see me in the field. The presence of their master and owner and protector put them at ease as nothing else could do, and this applied day and night." [4] Whenever the sheep see the shepherd, they quickly forget their rivalries and stop their fighting. There is nothing like the knowledge of Christ's presence to distill our own fear, panic and terror.

"As is the case with freedom from fear of predators or friction within the flock, the freedom of fear from the torment of parasites and insects is essential to the contentment of sheep. . . . Only the diligent care of the owner who keeps a constant lookout for these insects will prevent them from annoying his flock."[5] The Holy Spirit's anointing heals and restores us from the harsh realities of life. When we cry out to God, "Help me! This is too much and I can't take it," the Spirit helps us and applies the spiritual remedy to each of our situations.

The green pasture to which the shepherd guides his sheep does not just happen. According to Keller, these pastures are the product of tremendous labor, time and skill. They are the result of clearing rough rocky land, deep plowing, careful soil preparation, seeding, planting and irrigating. By skillful management and scientific land use, these parcels are soon converted and flourishing . . . so the flock can fill up quickly, then lie down quietly to rest and ruminate.[6] As sheep of the Good Shepherd, we are promised such a life. Christ works to clear our lives of rocky soil, bitter earth and hard-heartedness. He provides life-giving streams and proper pruning and cultivating. He cares for us so that we become fruitful and productive.

When sheep are thirsty, they become restless. The shepherd knows where the best drinking places are. If not led to the good water supplies of clean, pure water, sheep will often end up drinking from the polluted potholes where they pick up disease germs.[7] Sheep, by habit, rise just before dawn and start to feed. In these early hours, when grass and other vegetation are drenched with dew, sheep can become fully hydrated on the amount of water this dew provides. If we are devoted to following Christ daily, we will rise early each day and feed on God's Word. We will be satisfied by drinking from the fountain of life. Jesus said, "If any man thirst, let him come unto me and drink" (John 7:37, KJV). "Come, everyone who thirsts, / come to the waters; / and he who has no money, / come, buy and eat (Isa. 55:1). When we drink, we will be more confident and capable of dealing with the complex details of each day.

When David wrote Psalm 23, he knew what it was like to feel emotionally, physically and spiritually needy. He knew what it was like to feel hopeless and weak in his own strength. But he knew where to go to restore his soul. The Lord was his shepherd. In Psalm 42:11 (KJV) he cries out, "Why art thou cast down, O my soul? and why art thou disquieted within me?" He was in great distress, like a "cast" sheep lying on its back, legs in the air, frantically struggling but unable to raise itself. Without the Good Shepherd's ever-present watch over us plus His strength and help, you and I, as the cast sheep, will surely perish.

This ever-present danger is part of the pageantry and drama depicted for us in the magnificent story of the ninety-nine sheep and the one that went astray (see Matt. 18:12). "There is the shepherd's deep concern, his agonizing search, his longing to find the missing one, his delight in restoring it not only to its feet but also to the flock as well as to himself."[8] According to Keller, he would spend hours searching for the one missing sheep. More often than not, he would see it from a distance, lying helpless on its back. At once, he would run to it.

Within me there was a mingled sense of fear and joy: fear it might be too late; joy that it was found at all. . . . Tenderly I would roll the sheep over on its side. This would relieve the pressure of gases in the rumen. If she had been down for long, I would have to lift her onto her feet. Then, straddling the sheep with my legs, I would hold her erect, rubbing her limbs to restore the circulation to her legs. This often took quite a [bit of] time. . . . All the time I worked on the cast sheep, I would talk to it gently. . . . Little by little the sheep would regain its equilibrium. It would start to walk steadily and surely. By and by it would dash away to rejoin the others, set free from its fears and frustrations, given another chance to live a little longer. All of this pageantry is conveyed to my heart and mind when I repeat the simple statement, "He restoreth my soul!"[9]

Jesus has that same concern of mercy and compassion for "cast" men and women. It explains His benevolence to those treated unjustly and for whom society in His day (and ours) had no use. It reveals why He shed tears for those who rejected Him. It shows the depth of His love for those who need salvation.

"When the [sheep's] fleece becomes very long, and heavily matted with mud, manure, burrs and other debris, it is much easier for a sheep to become cast, literally weighed down with its own wool." Keller says, "Whenever I found that a sheep was being cast because it had too long and heavy a fleece, I soon took swift steps to remedy the situation. In short order I would shear it clean and so forestall the danger of having the ewe lose her life. This was not always a pleasant process."[10] Similarly, in dealing with our old selves, there will come a day when our Lord will discipline us and apply the sharp edge of His Word to our lives. At the time, it may prove a tough routine. But the truth is that this pruning will strengthen us and allow us to produce greater fruit.

AND YOU?

As you consider being a good neighbor, to whom is God leading you? How can you be a shepherd in your neighborhood and community? Where can you make the biggest difference? Whether you worship in the city, the suburbs or a rural area, there are many needs to be considered.

Consider those who are homeless, alcoholics and other drug addicts, those who are mentally disabled, migrant workers, the unemployed and working poor (underemployed), seniors and those who are illiterate. There are widowed men and women and those with chronic illness. How about those with special needs and people who are sight- and hearing-impaired and live in specialized care facilities? Have you considered single parents and their children or children in need of foster care? What about prison inmates or ex-offenders reentering society? There are also those women and children who are caught in the violence and abuse of sex trafficking and refugees/disaster victims and other immigrants.

Who are the members of your church or others who are lonely or timid or fearful? These are men and women who could easily "fall through the cracks" and disappear. In many cases, those who are missing may be cast down. You could be the one who finds and shepherds them in their home or elsewhere—even in the pews before or after church worship. You could be the one who brings to them hope and life. Pray for God's guidance in this regard.

Shepherding requires observation, keen eyesight and insight. As you look around during a church service, is anyone missing? Does anyone look like they are hurting or carrying a burden? Do you see anyone who looks sad or whose eyes are red? It doesn't take much to go to them and say something like, "Hi. We haven't met. My name is _____. Do you have a minute? I saw you by yourself and wanted to introduce myself." If you are concerned about someone you know who has been dealing with something difficult or has been ill, you can go to them and say, "Hi. I wanted to assure you of my continued prayer regarding such and such. How are you? I'm concerned." Because you have shown the other person that you are concerned, you've also shown that he or she is important to you. Shepherding makes a difference and allows for future ministry.

As good neighbors, we have many opportunities to shepherd others. In my own time of misery, when I made myself a prisoner in my apartment, God sent His shepherds—Christian friends who came to me when I was cast down. With God's help, they lifted me up and made sure I was recovering and okay. They led me in the paths of righteousness and made an eternal difference in my life.

Questions to Consider

1. Recall how someone shepherded you in the past. As a result, where did transformation take place in your life? Describe what it looked like. How can you use that experience for the benefit of others?

2. How can you lead someone to green pastures?

3. How can you lead someone to quiet waters?

4. How can you lead someone from the "valley" to blessedness?

9

LISTENING REVISITED: WHAT WE HEAR AND SAY

Years ago, as a child, I learned the importance of using words wisely. My nonreligious, Jewish parents taught me to use words in the right way. They said to me, "Do not hurt people with your words." They pretty much ingrained Ephesians 4:29 in my pre-Christian mind. "Let no corrupting talk come out of your mouths, but only such as is good for building up, as fits the occasion, that it may give grace to those who hear."

Their most notable instruction to me was not to use any ethnic or racial slurs. These were totally forbidden. And I honored that—that is, until the one time at age ten when I directed the n-word at a young, black child in my schoolyard. I was shocked that the word came out of my mouth. Nothing had provoked it. I did not know the other boy, and he did nothing to incur my wrath. I was taught not to say such a thing, yet I followed the similar patterns that I had heard other white kids use on the school playground. I say that I was shocked that the word came out of my mouth. But I was more shocked by the black child's response. He called me "white dog!" He responded in a way that he, too, probably learned from experience and observation. It was a stimulus-response action. My words hurt him, and he hurled hurtful words back. I had never been verbally assaulted before, and I felt crushed by his defensive attack. I immediately knew some of the disastrous effects of my ethnic slur on him. Possibly it was guilt and shame that caused me to feel as I did. Interestingly, this was so much worse than being on the receiving end of anti-Semitic attacks from those kids who hated Jews. Hearing kids call me "Jew boy" or "Hey kike" or "It looks like Hitler missed one" never affected me as much as this.

About the same time that I used the n-word, I listened to a favorite recording of the Broadway musical *South Pacific*, which features the song "You've Got to Be Carefully Taught."[1] I was so distraught that I never used that word ever again.

In considering much later in life why I attacked this person whom I did not know, it dawned on me that racism is as much a part of the American culture as fluoride is a part of our drinking water. We ingest it, not aware of its presence, and not even thinking about its effect on us. Hurtful words are so much a part of America's past and present history and are very much a part of common usage. Too many people continue to use ethnic and racial slurs and think racist thoughts. They are not being carefully taught; or they are being instructed, but they are not listening. Some ignore the apostle Paul's teaching to use only words that build up (see Eph. 4:29), while others have forgotten the words of the Golden Rule: "Do unto others what you want them to do unto you." They have not developed servant hearts and are not good neighbors or good listeners.

ETHICAL FORMATION

My parents were very active in the struggle for human rights. They were members of the Congress of Racial Equality (CORE) and were founders of "Panel of Americans," a forum for cross-cultural education and removal of racist stereotypes. My mother was a member of the Paterson, New Jersey Human Rights Commission. My father, who had a printing business, produced literature for the Anti-Defamation League, B'nai B'rith and other "brotherhood" organizations.

When I was a teenager, my rabbi, the Reverend Martin Freedman, participated in the southern Freedom Rides with other clergy. Along with others, he was jailed for protesting the politics and policies of segregation.[2] With his encouragement and support, and as a member of the National Federation of Jewish Youth, I was involved in protest marches; and I spoke publicly against segregation, racial discrimination, violence and murder in the southern states. Here is how the pastor by whom I was later discipled describes me in his book *Chains of Grace:*

> David was Jewish, living at home and attending his first year at a nearby college. He and Jim [a black teen] had become acquainted because Jim worked after school and on Saturdays in David's father's print shop. Harry, David's father, deeply believed the rightness of the civil rights struggle and wanted to do something to help. Jim began telling David about his church and the wonderful interracial fellowship there, and David got curious

enough to come that night. Because he loved the fellowship among the young people, he kept coming to church with Jim. After about a month he told me that he just didn't see the point of what I was teaching about Jesus. It wasn't that it antagonized him, but his response was rather, "So what?" Still, sitting through an hour of weekly irrelevance was a trade-off he was willing to make, so he continued to attend. . . . It all took place because an African-American teenaged Christian brought a socially conscious Jewish boy to a church where people were learning to live out the racial and social implications of the gospel.[3]

In the summer of 1965, my friend Jimmy (mentioned above) and I drove from our home in Paterson, New Jersey to see friends in Holland, Michigan who had just taught vacation Bible school at our church. Driving through Indiana we were pulled over by a state trooper. Jimmy was definitely guilty of "driving while black," and I was "driving with a black" and aiding and abetting a crime. Very quickly, two policemen got out of their car and told us to get out of our car. Then they separated us. I was standing by the car being questioned by one officer, while Jimmy was led perhaps fifty feet away and questioned by the other officer. That was the only similarity. The policeman who questioned me seemed relaxed. The policeman who questioned Jimmy seemed nervous and had his hand on his pistol the entire time. The only thing on my mind was the white and black civil rights activists who had been murdered recently (Andrew Goodman, James Chaney and Michael Schwerner, 1964; Viola Liuzzo, 1965). After a prolonged and frightening experience, the police—who did not seem interested in civil rights or racial justice—left us. When they were gone, Jimmy and I prayed, thanking God for hearing our silent cries for help. I was reminded of words we sang at church, "Lord, listen to your children praying; Lord, send your spirit to this place." He had listened to our unspoken prayers and responded.

OUR RESPONSE TODAY

Racial justice and reconciliation are essential building blocks to the church as a body and to its outreach. That, however, does not mean that our Asian, black, Latino and white members are reconciled to each other. Many tolerate people of other ethnicities and cultures and accept that the other is present. But there is little dialogue for mutual understanding. Because of this, the Tenth's Reconcilers Fellowship ministry was established to teach the church about and promote cross-cultural dialogue. It is a small group of men and women from diverse ethnic backgrounds who, with me, experienced a journey of discovery and community building.

Cross-cultural dialogue requires us to listen to our neighbors. It is spiritual in that it invites us to change our hearts and our behavior. And reconciliation asks us to live up to the high ideal of oneness that the Bible teaches. Galatians 3:28 says that we are all children of God through faith in Christ Jesus. "There is neither Jew nor Greek, there is neither slave nor free, there is no male and female, for you are all one in Christ Jesus." Reconciliation is more than tolerating our neighbor whose skin color is different from ours, because tolerance is not enough. Reconciliation encourages us to demonstrate love by accepting one another as brother and sister and listening to each other's stories.

A recent Urbana Missions Conference entitled "What Story Will You Tell?" focused on reconciliation. One of the speakers was Christena Cleveland who prayed a simple prayer before her talk: "Holy Spirit, we invite you to challenge us, to haunt us, to wreck our hearts for you." She then challenged everyone to see the injustice that continues to divide America into two or more Americas. She challenged us to come together, hear each other's stories and do something to address the parts of the body that are hurting. She challenged us to reach out to a neighbor and say, "Whatever life is like in your shoes, I want to know what that is" and "If you're saying that your life doesn't matter, tell me more."[4] If we want to be good neighbors, we can't address what we don't talk about. We won't understand unless we listen.

Attempting reconciliation gives testimony to the world what we followers of Jesus Christ believe—that in Him we are one (see Gal. 3:28). We are diverse, yet united. We are sinful, yet forgiven and working to be reconciled to one another. Given the history of racial strife in the American church, overcoming racial and ethnic divisions offers us the chance to show others our faith and our commitment by being obedient followers, good neighbors and good listeners. The fact that we demonstrate racial healing and unity shows others that Jesus Christ is the answer.

Tenth's Reconcilers Fellowship consisted of men and women from different upbringings. We were from segregated and integrated communities, urban and suburban, North and South. Our experiences were varied as well. For instance, one member, at a young age, witnessed a lynching in Georgia. Another member from Texas only had contact with people of color who were "the help"—the "girl" who did the laundry and the "boy" who did the gardening.

One member's family lived in a southern city and had more privileges than dark-skinned blacks because they had passed the "brown paper bag test." Two members who grew up in the North were involved in human rights activities and protest marches. And one member from Philadelphia feared daily the racism he would face because he woke up black. Our love of Christ and our love and respect for one another empowered us to share and listen to stories of shame and pain as we served as good neighbors to one another. We sought to bridge the cross-cultural and racial divide as we gathered together and listened to each other's stories. All of this took place prayerfully at the foot of the cross. These intentional conversations gave us a better handle on how to understand each other's life experience and heritage traditions. We listened to the stories in order to learn more and to more fully understand. We engaged in dialogue. We learned. We empathized. We offered hope. We established relationships. It can be done. You can do it too.

LISTENING AND CROSS-CULTURAL MINISTRY

Reconcilers Fellowship met over several months to discuss the idea of building up the church through a commitment to cross-cultural communication. The initial result was a three-day conference featuring Dr. John Perkins, president of the

Christian Community Development Association. The committee envisioned the conference as a bridge—the beginning of a process that would transform individual attitudes and develop greater listening capabilities. The immediate response was the desire for continued teaching on racism and reconciliation. We listened to the request, and the result was the first adult Bible class. The goals of this class were (1) to build bridges across the cross-cultural divide, (2) to grow in understanding of one another, (3) to encourage more cross-cultural relationships, and (4) to make our church and our homes places that create community and safe places to have interracial and cross-cultural dialogue.

The members of the first reconciliation class were eager to grapple with the topic, and prayer for the class and for one another was made part of the class as a rule. There were twelve in the original class: five African-Americans, six European-Americans, and myself (of Jewish heritage). The establishment of personal relationships was paramount. We wanted God to knit us together, people from diverse backgrounds and cultures, yet united as one. We wanted to heal wounds caused by racism and oppression. We wanted all who were involved—both those who had tasted and continue to taste the effects of racism, and those who had not and do not suffer—to be reconciled. Could we accomplish this?

There were lots of questions. There were lots of risks (anger, rejection, attack). Was Tenth Church ready? We reviewed where we were in Tenth's history. The Perkins/reconciliation conference was supported by the senior minister and the elders. As we listened to ourselves, we were confident that our process to be reconciled was biblical. This removed much of the burden we felt on our shoulders and helped us to pray for those people who might join us. We prayed that many minds and hearts would be changed. We prayed that many would grow to be better neighbors. We discovered that we, too, had to learn how to be better neighbors. Each of the committee members brought "baggage" to the table that affected our communication. For instance, when one member shared with tears about his grandmother's bitter and oppressive sharecropping experience, another member without thinking said, "That was a long time ago. You people need to let it go." Together, we listened to the immediate loud silence and witnessed the body language that showed anger, bewilderment and sadness. "You people should know your place is what I heard," was the response. "Your attitude harkens back to slavery and Jim Crow." No one spoke for a full minute. This was followed by a shameful acknowledgment of wrong and a plea for forgiveness by the offending party. We did not have it all together; yet we proceeded knowing that as we were cocreating this ministry together, we would also have to learn and grow together.

Making this journey required self-denial. There was also fear—fear of not being able to predict the outcome nor length of our experimental journey. All we knew was that the journey was necessary if we, and Tenth Presbyterian Church, were to grow. We were people wanting to take action who believed we had a practice field where it was safe to experiment.

One goal was to build community. We put this into action with a weekly adult Bible class on reconciliation and race, a monthly discussion forum for the committee itself and a monthly breakfast that featured guest speakers and group discussion.

ADULT BIBLE CLASS

For our adult Bible class, I prepared a class curriculum, a bibliography and ground rules for discussion. As already stated, one goal for this project was to develop a diverse community of believers and a safe place to dialogue on the topic of race and ethnicity.

The adult Bible class agreed to be a safe place to share feelings and experiences. The class would not be a pulpit for white folk to attack nonwhite folk, nor would any people of color use the class to launch any attacks of their own. The class would share, learn facts, learn about each other, learn how we should act as Christians and pray together. We began by asking two questions: "As a child, what were you taught about others?" and "As a child, what contact did you have with other ethnic groups?" These brought both similarities and differences to the table. Answers included: "I was raised in the South and was taught that I was better," "I have experienced subtle and overt racism from my childhood," and "I was taught that all folk were equal; but when I looked around, I knew that was not true." Most grew up in segregated areas, others in places of diversity. One person who grew up on army bases said she saw both separation and integration. Black class members shared how difficult the journey in a "white world" has been for them. Some also commented that they had a problem coming to Tenth—a "white church"—but continued because the teaching was good and sound. Another said that the mercy ministries made the church more credible. Blacks and whites agreed—the first class seemed to have gone well. The second week's discussion brought specific, hoped-for expectations:

prayer for church and city, sensitivity training, learning to change, working on prejudices and stereotypes, listening to one another and learning from each other. The class was seen as a plant that needed nurture and constant care. Racism was compared to the root system of a tree planted long ago that had now grown into the foundations of our homes. The roots needed to come out, and only a tree surgeon could do the job. The problem was that doing so would shake the foundations of our homes.[5] We focused on the history of white racism and the enslavement of African people in this country from the fifteenth century to the present. Exploring the facts of racism brought out mixed emotions from our members. Some African-Americans expressed anger and hostility, and some whites were in denial. Two black and three white members did not return to the second quarter of study for this reason. They wanted less talk and more action in the future.

The class continued with the core group, plus several others, with the topic of "Dismantling Racism," breaking down the walls that divide ethnic groups. The class sought to understand the process of biblical repentance and forgiveness. We discussed racial stereotypes and sinful perceptions—attitudes and behaviors toward various ethnic groups that need correction. Above all, we wanted to learn about each other and to build up one another in love.

NEW GROWTH

There was a new sense of belonging in the group. We did create a safe place where we could discuss tough issues. We began emptying ourselves of false presuppositions; and as we removed our masks, we became more honest and vulnerable. The group as a whole and as individuals were building and learning together. We were becoming family, seeking to love and build up one another. As a family, then, we asked the question, "Can we make this pilgrimage together, and if so, at what price?"

We studied *More Than Equals* by Spencer Perkins and Chris Rice, where the following discussion is found.

> Racial reconciliation is surgery, and surgery is never painless. Fear of this pain prompts many Christians to ignore their racial blinders. But the point where we feel pain is the beginning of the surgical process. . . . A doctor can't do open-heart surgery on you unless you're willing to get onto the operating table, allow him to cut beneath the skin and expose your most sensitive and vital organs to his healing knife. You do it only if you trust the surgeon. "Racial reconciliation," maintained Tom Skinner [evangelist and human rights advocate], "is whites and blacks holding on to each other, not letting go, and doing surgery on each other." Reconciliation requires exposing our vital organs to the truth that we speak to each other. It's risky. If trust hasn't been built, the operation is destined to fail. But when we build trust and stay on the table to the end of the surgery, there is hope for healing in the most delicate and vital places of our racial residue.[6]

It was at this time in our study that we began to gain the trust needed in the community-building effort to do that kind of spiritual surgery. We were maturing to the point of beginning to be "real" with one another.

In the third quarter, we added new members to the group. We discussed the videotape series *Let's Get to Know Each Other: What White and Black Christians Need to Know About Each Other* by Rev. Tony Evans.[7] Our agenda was to develop biblical attitudes and take steps toward relational healing. We recognized that we could not hope to resolve our problems with the philosophy and debate form of the world, but we could dissolve our differences beneath the cross of Christ. Yet, all of a sudden, seemingly out of nowhere, there were many frustrated comments. One white member complained about our process saying, "Let's stop talking and do something!" A black member was still wrestling with the history of racism at Tenth Church. "It wasn't until the mid-1960s that this church allowed blacks in," he said. While I wanted to rush in and rescue this situation, I felt that the comments were healthy and being shared in a safe place. That was our hope. No one was attacking anyone else. As we listened to and appreciated each other's stories, we were learning how to be good neighbors.

The next study was of Rev. Carl F. Ellis Jr.'s *Free at Last? The Gospel in the African-American Experience.* Mr. Ellis implores the church to develop a new urban paradigm—a biblical paradigm for today's needs. He criticizes both the liberal and conservative denominations for not being holistic and urges them to follow the centrality of Scripture. He speaks about "White Christianity-ism," a religion of human design that is not in keeping with the Christianity of Christ. Mr. Ellis also says that this Christianity-ism is a Christianity that has been polluted by the secular themes of our culture. It attempts to hold the gospel hostage.[8]

Ellis calls for a biblical balance of word and deed, focusing not on just the body or just the soul, but on body, soul and mind. Mr. Ellis quotes Dr. Martin Luther King.

> The gospel at its best deals with the whole man, not only his soul but also his body, not only his spiritual well-being, but also his material well-being. . . . A religion that professes a concern for the souls of men and is not equally concerned about the . . . social conditions that cripple them, is a spiritually moribund religion.[9]

Our pursuit of dialogue and understanding continued with the discussion of: *The Disease of Racism* by Terry Stull, *Purging Racism from Christianity* by Jefferson Edwards, and *Reconciliation: Our Greatest Challenge, Our Only Hope* by Curtiss Paul DeYoung. The study of each new title added to the strength of our community. We were also able to discuss our goals with the pastors and elders who now shared them.

MULTIETHNIC DIALOGUE BUILDS COMMUNITY

Several months after the adult Bible classes began, we initiated a monthly breakfast. These meetings, open to the public, featured speakers of various ethnicities. Topics included: Korean perspectives on race, Hispanic perspectives on race, confessions of a white racist, what it means to be black in a white culture, how to teach our children about racism, racism and church history, anti-Semitism, and others. Members of our group also participated in the Philadelphia edition of the National Dialogue on Race.

Another Tenth Church Urban Missions Conference entitled "What Does the Lord Require of You?" was held. The featured presenters were the Reverends Carl Ellis and Randy Nabors, who ministered cross-culturally in Chattanooga, Tennessee. The conference included workshops as well as keynote addresses on the main theme, and the "Racial Reconciliation from an African-American Perspective" seminar brought increased dialogue and confidence in our process of creating healthy cross-cultural relationships and community.

WHAT IS COMMUNITY?

A community is a group of people gathered together who are united in purpose, goals and vision. As a Christian community, we were willing to deny ourselves and learn from biblical examples.

In the Bible we read about this type of community in the book of Acts.

> And they devoted themselves to the apostles'
> teaching and the fellowship, to the breaking of
> bread and the prayers. And awe came upon every
> soul, and many wonders and signs were being done
> through the apostles. And all who believed were
> together and had all things in common. And they
> were selling their possessions and belongings and

> distributing the proceeds to all, as any had need. And day by day, attending the temple together and breaking bread in their homes, they received their food with glad and generous hearts, praising God and having favor with all the people. And the Lord added to their number day by day those who were being saved. (Acts 2:42–47)

Our attempt at developing community reflected the grace of God. In many ways it was mysterious, miraculous, inclusive, real, humble, self-giving, compassionate, welcoming and intimate. It was a safe place where we did not feel threatened. For most of those involved, it was rain needed by a plant in dry ground. And our community did not just happen. We built it over time—by tearing down walls and by building up good neighbor relationships.

We transformed feelings of alienation into feelings of appreciation, acceptance and humility. In this fledgling community, we shared a mutual brokenness that was genuine and real.

COMMUNITIES PROVIDE A WELCOME

We welcomed new people to the discussion process and developed trust as we listened to stories of past and current experiences with racism. We sought to model theologian Henri Nouwen's teaching that Old and New Testament stories not only show how serious our obligation is to welcome the stranger into our homes, but also tell us that guests are carrying precious gifts with them that they are eager to give to a receptive host.[10] The warmth of this welcoming provided for new people the spirit of healing from estrangement and alienation. They also shared our sense of brokenness, the need for each other for healing and the desire to grow in community.

Our community became a sacred space where safe conversation and listening could occur. We asked questions about deep and long-held presuppositions and beliefs. "Is what I was taught by my family and practiced by those around me actually true?" "Why do I believe and think the way I do about blacks, Jews, Poles, Italians and Chinese?" "Why do whites and people of color think the way they do?" We stuck our necks out continuously and learned from each experience. We answered the questions and constructed new bridges strengthened by listening and being good neighbors.

COMMUNITY BUILDING IS NOT ALWAYS COMFORTABLE

Our new community was in uncharted waters. Yet we had the building blocks to create change found in Philippians 2 ("Have the mind of Christ"). We were prayerfully seeking God's will for direction, building each other up, being careful and sensitive to the effects of the process. We were creating a paradigm shift. We were changing our worldview—the way we perceived the world. We were seeking a biblical worldview, a scriptural filter to live by. We were working against opposing views that said, "That's impossible," "That's not the way we do things around here," "We've never done it that way before," or "We tried that before and it didn't work." We were pioneers and catalysts, people who took risks and would not settle for the status quo. We began the process thinking we were community by virtue of the fact that we met together. We were not. These were clearly uncharted waters. In the beginning, our individual differences were very visible, and some of us felt uncomfortable. We, of course, wanted comfort as we listened to other views and experiences that were different from our own. Our ancestors came from Africa, Asia, Europe and Russia. Some of us grew up in the South (below the Mason-Dixon Line); others grew up in the North (urban and suburban). Some were privileged; others suffered from oppression. Some felt the pain of racism and ethnic prejudice.

Nothing we did fit in a nice, tidy box. In fact, there was no box. We were in a laboratory experimenting with hazardous materials that could explode at any time. Honest discussion was difficult. Words and attitudes that were expressed caused pain. It was a time of creative, constructive sharing, and it was unpleasant at times. But we were working toward a goal. In that there was no division.

We faced crises. But they were healthy. (In the Chinese language, the English word crisis consists of two characters, one representing danger and the other hidden opportunity.) The danger of anger was limited by how we told the truth in love and how we listened with love. There were no more blow-ups because we were working toward Christian community. We were becoming conscious of our prejudices and were ready to empty ourselves of them.

OPPORTUNITY FOR US . . . AND YOU

Being able to "empty" ourselves of racially charged, false presuppositions was a pleasant surprise. As we listened to one another—putting those presuppositions on the table—and prayed together, we were blessed. Our work as good neighbors bore the fruit of healing and unity. The emptying freed us to be more open and vulnerable. Purging ourselves of presuppositions and recognizing racial stereotypes helped us be freer to share and more eager to listen.

Because we grew in relationships of trust, we could be transparent. Trust allowed us to do "spiritual surgery" to cleanse the racist infection (attitudes and behaviors), along with the post-op work of recovery. You might say there was a rebirth of servant hearts and minds. More and more we enjoyed unity in our diversity. In the process, we developed community and a model for what you, with others, can accomplish. In the appendix of this book, entitled "Additional Tools and Resources," is the last of the guides that Tenth's Reconcilers Fellowship used for our conversations on race. I discovered that someone else had developed a guide to build cross-cultural bridges, so I didn't have to.[11] It helped us to acknowledge that we need to be aware that racism exists past and present, that we are willing to discuss it honestly, that we are repentant and that we are able to forgive our brothers and sisters. I include it hoping you will find it useful.

Toward the end of Tenth Presbyterian's own Reconcilers Fellowship's last session, we read part of the children's book *The Velveteen Rabbit*. In the book is a conversation between a child and his toy and an answer to the question, "What is REAL?"

> "Real isn't how you are made," said the Skin Horse.
> "It's a thing that happens to you. When a child
> loves you for a long, long time, not just to play with,

but REALLY loves you, then you become Real."
"Does it hurt?" asked the Rabbit. "Sometimes," said
the Skin Horse, for he was always truthful. "When
you are Real, you don't mind being hurt." "Does it
happen all at once, like being wound up," he asked,
"or bit by bit?" "It doesn't happen all at once," said
the Skin Horse. "You become. It takes a long time.
That's why it doesn't often happen to people who
break easily, or have sharp edges, or who have to be
carefully kept. Generally, by the time you are Real,
most of your hair has been loved off, and your eyes
drop out and you get loose in the joints and very
shabby. But these things don't matter at all, because
once you are Real, you can't be ugly, except to people who don't understand."[12]

Although meant for children, this reading had us reflect
on the process of our becoming REAL with one another. As
the story goes, we are "becoming." And yes, it does take a long
time.

Our Reconciler's Fellowship ministry no longer exists in
its official capacity. Most of the members left to be part of a
church plant. Others simply moved on to other outreach, still
utilizing what they learned. But Tenth continues its journey
in listening and being reconciling neighbors. The books we
used, along with others, are in the church's library. I continue
to be a cheerleader and a catalyst for reconciliation at Tenth
and elsewhere. As I write this, a "Reconciliation" motion has
been passed by my denomination, the Presbyterian Church in
America. These pastors and elders listened to their brothers

and sisters of color and will continue, as good neighbors, to do so. I am interested in seeing how the process goes and how God creates servant hearts in his people.

Questions to Consider

1. What racist presuppositions do you need to get rid of? How will you accomplish this?

2. Do your friends include people of color? Why or why not? What would you change and how?

3. Are you listening to those who are affected by racism? If so, how. If not, why not?

4. Describe the risk taken by Reconcilers Fellowship to develop unity. What did you learn?

5. What did you think of the "Guide for Conversations on Race" in the back of this book? How would you put it into practice? Who will help you?

10

DEVELOPING HEALTHY BOUNDARIES
IN THE BODY OF CHRIST

Christ invites His followers to welcome those on society's margins, including people with mental illness and other disabilities. When we do so, we need strategies to keep their needs from overwhelming us. Congregations are sometimes less than welcoming to certain people out of fear that "needy people" will burn out their caring capacities. It is easy to avoid people whose behavior we do not understand. Yet we are members of one another (see Eph. 4:25) who suffer as a body when one member suffers (see 1 Cor. 12:26). We are called to care for hurting people among us and around us. Boundaries enable us to persist in sharing Christ's love through difficult circumstances.[1] Most of us know or come into contact with people inside and outside our churches who do not know how to set limits for themselves or who are manipulative and push the limits of others. Their decisions usually have hurtful or unhealthy consequences. That is why it is so important that we develop healthy boundaries.

Here are two illustrations that highlight this point.

Not long ago, I received a call from a deaconess at another church. She spoke about a particular case, asked if she had done the right thing, and wondered what I would do in a similar situation. This is what the deaconess said: "A woman called me several weeks ago at my home. She is not a member of our church, and I do not know her. I don't know how she got my name and phone number, but she called me asking for help. She sounded very upset and told me that her daughter has leukemia and is in the hospital. According to the woman, most of their income is going toward medical bills, and they have been threatened with eviction. They could really use the help of our church. I took her phone number and told her I would respond as soon as I could."

The deaconess told me that she phoned back the following day and discovered that there is no such phone number. She tried again and again—even changing one of the numbers in case she had written it down wrong—but the answer was the same. There is no such number. The deaconess then tried the hospital to learn of the daughter's condition and was told that they could not give out that information. Undeterred, the deaconess went to the hospital the following day to visit the daughter (and with hope of meeting the mother who had called). When she arrived at the information counter, the deaconess stated that she was from such and such a church to visit this particular patient. The deaconess was surprised once again when told that there was no such patient.

I asked the deaconess, "How much time did you give to this matter?" "Hours" was the answer. "How much anxiety did you feel in the service?" I asked. "Much" was the answer. "How do you feel about the entire episode" I asked? "I am saddened by it all. I feel like I wasted my time."

As the deaconess and I spoke to evaluate how she had responded to the caller, she saw that she was unwise in rushing to action without thinking about the request clearly. She saw that she needed better boundaries in order to avoid repeating her "tyranny of the urgent" response.

On another occasion, a deacon was assigned a particular case. A church member approached him and stated that his expenses—as little as they were—were greater than his income. Neither the deacon nor the church member had boundaries. The deacon helped pay the member's bills over a period of months only to discover that the member had a gambling addiction, which is what caused the problem—he actually lost his earnings at the racetrack. When the deacon discovered the cause, he became so angry when he saw the member in church that he tried to choke him with his hands. It was quite a sight. The deacon's lack of boundaries and the demands made on him were destructive to future ministry. In his particular case, he did not understand the need for boundaries and declared that he had done nothing wrong. He left his church for another not long after this incident.

INCLUDING, NOT MARGINALIZING

Most of us know someone who makes frequent demands that must be met NOW! They seem to live in perpetual crisis and not recognize that others have needs too. In congregations, such people may find themselves excluded and on the margins when caring people become resentful and exhausted.

If we find a brother or sister in the church who is demanding or difficult, we need to remember that part of the difficulty always lies with us. When we notice our frustration, anger and resentment growing, it is a signal to listen to the Holy Spirit urging us to pay special attention to the relationship. How do we respond with the love of Christ so that we can include them and not allow resentment to have the upper hand?

CULTIVATING COMPASSIONATE RESPECT

A response that embodies the compassion of Christ may come easier if we cultivate empathy. People who demand a disproportionate share of a congregation's resources are often dealing with multiple pressing issues all at once—for example, disability (including mental illness), relationship stress, financial crisis, addiction, discrimination, trauma, etc. The need to ask for help is an added stress factor. Our compassionate respect for people who struggle can grow if we consider that most are doing the best that they can with whatever is available to them. It may also help to understand that manipulation may be the only way they know to get legitimate needs met. Expressing our appreciation for how well they are coping with immense challenges may be a way to put relationships on a good footing. This is especially helpful when we face the need to set firm boundaries.

BOUNDARY SETTING

Healthy boundaries allow us to be effective and maintain relationships across time. Setting boundaries requires us to be aware of where our responsibilities end and those of others begin. We need a strong sense of self in order to differentiate between requests that are appropriate and those that are not.

In each situation we need to evaluate the relative importance of three areas:

- our relationship with the other person

- our objectives (getting what we want)

- our self-dignity or self-respect

When someone is demanding of us, we need to determine which of these three areas is most important at the moment and respond accordingly. We will likely have difficulty setting healthy boundaries if we find ourselves always focusing on the same area.

Suppose we always give in to demands from a certain person in our congregation in order to maintain the relationship. This sacrifices our own or congregational objectives and our self-respect. We are teaching the person, inadvertently, that they are entitled to ask for whatever they want and receive it. This pattern will make it difficult to say no, even when a request clearly interferes with our self-respect or the best interests of others and the congregation as a whole.

Alternatively, if we always make a priority of getting our own or congregational needs met, then the person making the request will feel run over or ignored. When this happens often, the person will not experience the blessing that comes from inclusion in the body of Christ. Maintaining balance between the three approaches allows us flexibility in compassionately responding to people. We can more readily set boundaries needed for the well-being of all.

RESPONDING THOUGHTFULLY

Responding too quickly to those who place demands on us often grows out of anxiety. When we feel on the spot, cornered or out of our league, anxiety may push us to respond right away. Complying immediately with the request may relieve tension for the moment but lead to later regret.

Here are some suggestions that will decrease anxiety:

- Take a deep breath.

- Pray.

- Feel your feet close to the earth.

- Try to evaluate all the conditions of the request.

- Ask for time to come to an answer.

- Step out of the room and reenter.

Responding thoughtfully in the face of "NOW demands" requires us to know our own needs, desires and limits. We need an intact sense of self-respect. We must also commit ourselves to remaining in relationship with the ones making demands on us. The reward for such hard, inclusive work is a chance to benefit from God's amazing gifts hidden in people we might have otherwise written off with the label "difficult."

WHAT DO DIFFICULT PEOPLE LOOK LIKE?

They are needy, demanding, controlling and arrogant. Some may have damaged emotions and carry much pain. Difficult people can be manipulative and skilled at moving us to act as they wish us to act. They might use guilt to manipulate us, or they might make it seem that we have a responsibility to help them.

Difficult people are hard to get along with and difficult to work with (despite the need to do so). They have a pattern of making poor choices and find it difficult to change (or refuse to accept the fact that healthier skills are needed). They are unreasonable and uncooperative. They tend to be aggressive—perhaps bullying, contentious and highly critical.

Some difficult people come out charging. They can be openly aggressive, pushy and abrupt. They can show disapproval and seek to humiliate people—sometimes publicly. It is not unusual for difficult people to show rage and "have a tantrum."

The following discussion on healthy boundaries has been adapted from an article by Christine Guth entitled "Healthy Boundaries in the Body of Christ."

WHY SET BOUNDARIES?

Among other benefits, boundaries allow us to risk opening our congregations to people with interesting challenges.

One metaphor for personal boundaries likens them to a fence surrounding our property. This fence helps us to know where our responsibilities begin and where they end. Setting limits does not mean that we are intolerant or selfish. It means that we are protecting ourselves from harm. It means we respect our own beliefs, feelings and actions, and we take good care of ourselves. We need boundaries when we care for hurting people. We will not be able to help others if our own needs are great (or if we lack boundaries). In order to sustain proper care for ourselves, our physical, emotional and spiritual resources must be constantly replenished.

WHAT DO HEALTHY BOUNDARIES LOOK LIKE?

HEALTHY BOUNDARIES INVOLVE A REALISTIC ASSESSMENT OF OUR OWN ABILITIES AND SHORTCOMINGS

- Having an honest view of ourselves, not a grandiose view that we are irreplaceable

- Knowing that when we are exhausted or resentful, we are of little use to anyone

- Calling in more expertise when the situation exceeds our abilities

- Choosing which risks we will take on; risking someone's anger may be a better choice than risking the end of the relationship or someone's safety

- Having a backup plan ready to go in case things don't go as hoped

- Accepting the support we need when we are bearing others' burdens and setting limits

- Paying attention to the stress our caregiving for others places on our family

HEALTHY BOUNDARIES INVOLVE A REALISTIC VIEW OF THE OTHER

- Providing opportunities and expectations that fit that person's abilities and gifts

- Avoiding unintended exclusion by setting the bar too high for that person (easy to do if we don't understand a disability well)

- Being alert to any history of abusive behavior and preventing circumstances that might give opportunity for further abuse

HEALTHY BOUNDARIES INVOLVE CONTROLLING WHAT WE DO, NOT WHAT THE OTHER PERSON DOES

Often we begin setting boundaries by deciding on what we think are appropriate and sustainable ways of relating. Then we spell these out in expectations for the other person. But stating expectations is only the first step of setting limits. The second step, indispensable but often neglected, is to decide on a plan of response if or when the person is unwilling or unable to meet our expectations. Our plan must involve only actions we have control over, only actions we are willing to implement.

HEALTHY BOUNDARIES INVOLVE LETTING GO

Despite how it may look at first glance, we do not set boundaries in order to hoard energy, time or resources for ourselves. Rather than clinging to resources, we are letting go of attempts to control the other person and the situation. We are releasing things over which we have no control. Letting go is possible when we trust that God is in control, so we do not have to be. As we let go of control, we will likely also need to let go of worry about what other people think about our actions. We may even need to limit our contact with others who disapprove of our boundary setting.

HEALTHY BOUNDARIES INVOLVE MODELING SELF-CARE AND RESPECT FOR OTHERS

These are qualities we hope to encourage in those we care for. If we give too much without making our needs known, others will not know when they are hurting us. Our boundaries must also have roots in respect for the dignity of the other and in knowledge that someday we too will need care.

HEALTHY BOUNDARIES INVOLVE SHARING ENOUGH INFORMATION WITH THOSE WHO NEED TO KNOW

People affected by a challenging behavior set better limits when they hear from those who know the person best. This could be parents, a case manager or other professionals. Such sharing naturally depends on obtaining the person's permission. On the other hand, someone may tend to share too much in the wrong setting. Leaders might encourage a person to limit sharing to those who need to know. This may reduce problems that could arise when others do not have the full context. Designating a circle of support in a congregation can sometimes give more stable support to a person with mental illness. Responding to needs can be more coordinated when all members of the caring circle share the same information. The team approach allows those setting limits to draw on the wisdom of others as they decide when and where to place a boundary. Those not in the circle can trust that care is being provided.

HEALTHY BOUNDARIES INVOLVE ACKNOWLEDGING WHEN WE CAUSE HURT

Sometimes the limits we set will feel hurtful to another person. Such hurt may be unavoidable at times. When we anticipate this, we might say something like, "We want to care for you and be your brothers and sisters, but we can't do it perfectly; we are going to fail. I'm sorry."

HEALTHY BOUNDARIES INVOLVE ADJUSTING TO CHANGING CIRCUMSTANCES

We need to be ready to shift our boundaries as needs change. If looser limits are not working, we may need to think about moving the boundary to a more restrictive place. Signs of growth may allow us to relax boundaries that are no longer needed.

HARD WORK

Healthy boundaries involve hard work when we are motivated by caring and empathy. Ironically, we often expend just as much energy when we *avoid* setting boundaries. Taking on responsibilities that do not belong to us is draining. This is often a misguided effort to protect others from hurt feelings or natural consequences. We may attempt to control others, when all we can really control is ourselves. As a result, we find ourselves stuck. We repeatedly make the same responses to behaviors, even when they get us nowhere. When this happens, it is a clear signal to reevaluate where our responsibilities begin and end. Then we need to change our actions accordingly.

WELCOMING THOSE WHOM CHRIST HAS INVITED

For the strength and insight to set and live within boundaries, we depend on the source of all strength, God's all-sufficient grace. When our boundaries are well cared for, we are able to protect the well-being of each person in a relationship. They allow us choices in life. They provide guidance, pointing out what benefits or harms the relationship as a whole. Our boundaries help us make adjustments in the relationship to forestall extreme events—events that might force change and damage or sever the relationship. In these ways our boundaries are strategies that help us welcome those in Christ's body whom Christ Himself has invited.[2]

REMINDER: FENCES PROTECT

Strong boundaries help us avoid unnecessary pain and discomfort. They are like tall, sturdy fences with a gate, a latch and a secure lock that controls who is allowed to come and go. Boundary fences are not impenetrable, but they do not allow people to roam about freely either. The best boundaries feature a locked gate. It isn't enough to have a gate that is merely latched. And it isn't enough to have a lock without actually locking it. We alone hold the key that unlocks the lock and permits select people to enter into our lives. If we don't control our lives by protecting our boundaries, we are fair game for long-lasting injury. Proverbs 25:28 states well that "man without self-control is like a city broken into and left without walls."

JESUS SET BOUNDARIES

Our Savior protected Himself too. He had far more stress, far more pressure and far more responsibility than any of us; yet He remained relaxed, joyful and generous with people. His ability to care for Himself wisely prevented Him from becoming overwhelmed or burning out. Jesus' lifestyle is a model for us. While He showed us how to serve others, His spirit of love and self-control was evident. He did not allow people to use Him as a doormat. Jesus doesn't call us to be doormats either. By observing His lifestyle, we can see how to be better neighbors with healthy boundaries.

In His humanity, Jesus had limitations that He accepted in a relaxed way: like being in a human body that needed nourishment and rest and could only be in one place at a time; or like there being only twenty-four hours in a day. Jesus had personal priorities that He put over the needs of others—and He did so without feeling guilty. In order to care for Himself, He often separated Himself from people to be alone with God. Jesus' lifestyle protected Him from burn out and kept Him spiritually strong so that He could be merciful in His response to people, their needs, interruptions and crises.

Jesus did not overextend or completely exhaust Himself before finally taking a break. Instead, He proactively invested in intimacy with His Father, which gave Him greater energy and focus. Because He understood the need for physical, emotional and spiritual rest, He never burned out.

When people were demanding, He didn't always do what they wanted Him to do. There were many people He did not help. And when He did help others, He expected them to do their part. For instance, the blind man had to walk a long way to get to the pool of Siloam to wash the mud out of his eyes (see John 9:7). These understandings teach us how to speak the truth in love and how to live within our personal limitations.

Jesus had basic needs too. He ate healthy foods, got the sleep He needed (even took naps), took time to relax and did a lot of walking (see Matt. 26:18-20; John 12:2). He sought the company of friends and, when necessary, withdrew from crowds to be alone with His Father or with friends (see Matt. 26:36–38; Luke 5:16). He was never in a hurry, except to go to Jerusalem and face the cross (see Mark 10:32–34). Jesus was tempted to become paralyzed with fear about the cross. Satan and his demons, along with many people who hated Jesus, were trying to kill Him. He chose not to force things, but to trust His Father's will for the suffering and trials to come (see Mark 14:32-42). He did not allow others to control him. He said no to Herod's mocking demand to show him a sign that He was the Son of God (see Luke 23:8–9). He didn't give in to His mother and brothers who tried to use their relationship with Him to pull Him away (see Matt. 12:46–50). And, when the religious leaders asked Him baiting questions to make Him look foolish, He answered with incisive questions of His own (see 21:23–27; 22:15–22).

JESUS' BOUNDARIES FOR US

Make time for personal prayer: "But when you pray, go into your room, close the door and pray to your Father, who is unseen" (Matt. 6:6, NIV).

Be honest and direct: "Simply let your 'Yes' be 'Yes,' and your 'No,' 'No.' Anything more comes from the evil one" (5:37, BSB).

Set priorities: "No servant can serve two masters. Either he will hate the one and love the other, or he will be devoted to the one and despise the other" (Luke 16:13, BSB).

Please God, not people: "How can you believe since you accept glory from one another but do not seek the glory that comes from the only God?" (John 5:44, NIV).

Obey God: "There was a man who had two sons. He went to the first and said, 'Son, go and work today in the vineyard.' 'I will not,' he answered, but later he changed his mind and went. Then the father went to the other son and said the same thing. He answered, 'I will, sir,' but he did not go. Which of the two did what his father wanted?" "'The first,' they answered"

(Matt. 21:28–31, niv).[3] Jesus set boundaries. He visited, listened and healed—physically and spiritually. He calls us to do the same. He calls us to develop servant hearts and to be good neighbors.

PUT IT INTO PRACTICE

The spiritual warfare I faced while writing this book and the angst I described in the introduction brought me to the foot of the cross again and again and again. I praise God for continuously restoring my soul and leading me in the right paths to follow Jesus, develop the heart of a servant and be a good neighbor.

Consider those who are homeless, those who are alcoholics or drug addicts, those who are mentally disabled, migrant workers, the unemployed and working poor (underemployed), seniors, and those who are illiterate. There are widowed men and women and those with chronic illness. How about those with special needs, people who are sight and hearing impaired, and those who live in specialized care facilities? Have you considered single parents and their children? Or children in need of foster care? What about prison inmates or ex-offenders reentering society? There are also women and children who are caught in the violence and abuse of sex trafficking, refugees and disaster victims, and other immigrants.

Who do you know who needs a caring neighbor, a listening ear, a softly spoken word, a gentle touch or some encouragement? Go to them. In the name of Jesus, minister to them. All the how-to answers lie in the ways of Jesus and how He demonstrated the heart of a servant. If only we could demonstrate this way of life in word and deed. Our Lord has set forth good neighbor principles in Scripture. The problem is not that the principles don't work, but that they are so rarely practiced. Putting Christ first and dethroning ourselves are the first and required steps for everyone in every congregation.

Questions to Consider

1. How do you relate to the deaconess' "tyranny of the urgent" tale? Describe a similar personal experience.

2. Describe your own boundaries or lack of boundaries. How has this chapter helped you?

3. What did you learn about Jesus' boundaries that helped you? Which ones did you appreciate the most and are now planning to put into practice?

APPENDIX:

ADDITIONAL TOOLS AND RESOURCES

TENTH PRESBYTERIAN'S RECONCILERS' FELLOWSHIP
A GUIDE FOR CONVERSATIONS ON RACE

INTRODUCTION

Are you someone who:

- Is heartbroken by the racial divide you see in your country, your city, your church, your family?

- Wants to experience greater diversity and richness in your relationships?

- Wants the church to demonstrate God's heart for diversity to the world?

- Feels fearful and awkward toward knowing how to connect with others of a different race?

The Reconciliation Journey is Not an Easy Process

It can be daunting and scary to launch into the unknown abyss of racial conversations. It takes brave people to have courageous conversations. You may be like me; as you look around at the many racial divides, you want to do something. We have read the Scriptures; we have prayed for unity. But how do we, the body of Christ, work out the process of becoming one? How do God's words come alive and live in each of us? How does unity begin to permeate our entire being? How do we become light to a dark world that makes and accepts racial divisions? How does the body of Christ become a witness and a voice for unity? The purpose of this conversation is to help us get unstuck. It is designed as the first step in relational unity, through communication that will lead to understanding and healing.

Our goals are:

- To glorify God

- To promote greater unity in the body of Christ

- To show evidence of Christians authentically being healed and transformed at the foot of the cross

What we need:

- Humility and openness to learn

- Vulnerability

- Willingness to trust God as we engage

- Commitment to the process

Speaking the truth in love, we will:

- Communicate the big picture.

- Give the history of Tenth's process, that is, what we talked about.

- Briefly introduce ourselves to one another.

- Say why we are here and what we hope to gain.

- Establish trust. Commit ourselves to listening to and sharing with others for the purpose of building up, not tearing down.

Scriptures:

- Galatians 3:28 – "There is neither Jew nor Greek, there is neither slave nor free, there is no male and female, for you are all one in Christ Jesus."

- 2 Corinthians 5:17–21 – "Therefore, if anyone is in Christ, he is a new creation. The old has passed away; behold, the new has come. All this is from God, who through

Christ reconciled us to himself and gave us the ministry of reconciliation; that is, in Christ God was reconciling the world to himself, not counting their trespasses against them, and entrusting to us the message of reconciliation. Therefore, we are ambassadors for Christ, God making his appeal through us. We implore you on behalf of Christ, be reconciled to God. For our sake he made him to be sin who knew no sin, so that in him we might become the righteousness of God."

AWARENESS

"Awareness" is generally defined as the state or condition of being aware; having knowledge; consciousness. In order for transformation to occur, we must realize our need to be reconciled to one another. According to Latasha Morrison, the Duke Center for Reconciliation defines "reconciliation" as "God's initiative, restoring a broken world to His intentions by reconciling to Himself all things through Christ: the relationship between people and God, between people themselves, and with God's created Earth. Christians participate with God by being transformed into ambassadors of reconciliation."[1]

Discussion Questions:

- Describe the most important experience that shaped you into the person you are today.

- Describe something you love about your own culture and something you wish was different.

- Describe a time when someone of another culture made an assumption about your culture, and it caused you harm. How did you respond?

- Why does building a relationship with someone of a different race matter so much?

- What difference would it make (in our friendships, our families, our community, the broader current culture, etc.) if diversity was more of a reality?

- How can we ensure that this conversation today doesn't end here but continues and becomes part of our lives?

- In a single sentence, using the beginning statement "I WILL . . ." please share what YOU are willing to do to help make the church one in which assumptions and prejudgment don't affect OUR relationships with one another.

Scriptures:

- Ephesians 2:14–6 – "For he himself is our peace, who has made us both one and has broken down in his flesh the dividing wall of hostility by abolishing the law of commandments expressed in ordinances, that he might create in himself one new man in place of the two, so making peace, and might reconcile us both to God in one body through the cross, thereby killing the hostility."

Prayer:

> Lord, make us ambassadors of reconciliation. Give us your eyes of awareness; open our ears that we may hear you. Allow us to see others as you see them. Teach us to speak your words of truth and forgiveness. Transform our hearts so we may bring wholeness to those that are broken. Lord, use us to tear down the barriers that continue to divide your body. Amen

ACKNOWLEDGMENT

Acknowledgment leads us, as believers, to practice lamenting. Lamenting is when we express regret or disappointment over something considered unsatisfactory, unreasonable or unfair. This may be attitudes others have about us or things they've done to us.

It can also be sinful things we ourselves have said and done. We must acknowledge our own brokenness and the brokenness of others. We must acknowledge the racial divide and injustices that plight our nation. We must acknowledge our part in the issue and our part in the resolution.

Discussion Questions:

- Describe a time when you wrongly assumed something about someone. Describe how it made you feel.

- Describe a time someone wrongly assumed something about you. Describe how it made you feel.

- How has race affected your faith?

- Tell a story about racism. When did you first feel its effects or observe it?

- Do you believe that, despite its frequent missteps, the church is the one institution that is best equipped to overcome the racial divide?

Scriptures:

- 1 John 1:9 – "If we confess our sins, he is faithful and just to forgive us our sins and to cleanse us from all unrighteousness."

- Isaiah 1:18 (KJV) – "Come now, and let us reason together, saith the LORD: though your sins be as scarlet, they shall be as white as snow; though they be red like crimson, they shall be as wool."

Prayer:

> Lord, thank you for making us aware of our ignorance and apathy. Thank you for allowing us to be a part of this discussion. Lord, help us to acknowledge our responsibility for racial reconciliation. Reveal both our weaknesses and our strengths so that we may be credible witnesses of the gospel. Thank you for being a God who is mighty to save and able to do what we ourselves cannot. Amen

SHAME AND GUILT

The process of reconciliation may include a season of shame and guilt. As we process injustice and racism, plus our and others' brokenness, feelings of guilt and shame may arise. Some of us have been affected by our family members' ungodly views on race. Those family members may be Christians with inherited beliefs. Personal and systemic racism requires the same forgiveness-of-sin process—awareness, confession and repentance—as any other sin. We need to pray for our relatives. Be careful not to use Scripture as a sledgehammer, allowing shame and guilt (and Satan) to guide our actions. We cannot force true reconciliation. God is sovereign over the timetable.

Discussion Questions:

- What are some racial stereotypes, both positive and negative, that you've grown up with? How do you address prejudiced comments made by friends?

- What experiences of prejudices have you had in your family? Do you find it more difficult to address family issues of racism?

- How have family dynamics affected your perspective on race?

- What prejudices toward others do you need to release?

Scriptures:

- James 5:16 (NIV) – "Therefore, confess your sins to each other and pray for each other so that you may be healed."

CONFESSION

John R.W. Stott wrote in *Confess Your Sins*, "We reveal not the depth of our love, but its shallowness, for we are doing what is not for His highest good. Forgiveness which bypasses the need for repentance issues not from love but from sentimentality."[2]

Confession is the first step to repentance. It is difficult because it begins within a heart of humility (broken and contrite). We are all loved by Christ and justified through grace. We all sin and do things that are dishonoring or displeasing to God. Our sins disrupt our fellowship with God and others. Confessing those sins leads to a pathway of forgiveness and mends our broken fellowship.

Discussion Questions:

- How has the Lord transformed your heart?

- What two heart changes do you still want to see the Lord make?

- How has your family's history influenced your beliefs about race?

- What do you find most difficult in confessing your sins on racial relationships?

Scriptures:

- Isaiah 43:25 (NIV) – "I, even I, am he who blots out your transgressions, for my own sake, and remembers your sins no more."

- Matthew 6:14–15 (NIV) – "For if you forgive other people when they sin against you, your heavenly Father will also forgive you. But if you do not forgive others their sins, your Father will not forgive your sins."

Prayer:

> Father, we confess to you our blindness. We have not seen or felt the ways in which our actions or LACK OF ACTION may have contributed to hurting others. We confess our inattention to the things that matter so much to you. We confess our numbness and the ways we neglect to love others. Help us! We need to know You and our neighbor better. Amen

FORGIVENESS

Extending grace to those who have hurt us can be a hard task. But, forgiveness is a divine act. To forgive does not mean we have chosen to simply ignore or gloss over the evil and injustice we experienced or committed. It is realizing that Christ died to erase our sins. He suffered and paid for our sins to identify with the injustice and evil we have experienced. We are all guilty and in need of forgiveness. We forgive because we have been forgiven.

In the process of spiritual growth, we are being transformed into the likeness of Christ. This process does not happen overnight. But, as we mature, we must be gracious; we must listen; we must embrace others with a heart of compassion.

"Forgiveness is not an occasional act, it is a constant attitude." — Martin Luther King Jr.[3]

Discussion Questions:

- Why must we forgive?

- Why is forgiveness for us and not for the person you are forgiving?

- How do I forgive myself?

- What characteristics in our lives might indicate that we have not fully forgiven past hurts?

Scriptures:

- 2 Corinthians 5:17 – "Therefore, if anyone is in Christ, he is a new creation. The old has passed away; behold, the new has come."

- 2 Corinthians 7:10 (NIV) – "Godly sorrow brings repentance that leads to salvation and leaves no regret, but worldly sorrow brings death."

REPENTANCE

Repentance calls us to turn—from sin and to God. Repentance requires that we take a whole new point of view and leads us to genuine faith.

A.W. Tozer said, "Let us beware of vain and overhasty repentance, and particularly let us beware of no repentance at all. We are a sinful race . . . and until the knowledge has hit hard, until it has wounded us, . . . it has done us no good. A man can believe in total depravity and never have any sense of it for himself at all. Lots of us believe in total depravity who have never been wounded with the knowledge that we've sinned. Repentance is a wound I pray we may all feel."[4]

Discussion Questions:

- What do you think Tozer means by being "wounded with the knowledge that we've sinned?"

- What is the greatest hindrance or barrier to change?

- Why are we blind to our sins but we can easily see the sin of others?

- What are ideologies from childhood about race of which you need to let go?

- Why is true repentance so difficult?

Prayer:

> God, we thank you for producing a grief in us over our sins that then leads us to repentance. Your forgiveness toward us who don't deserve it empowers us to forgive others. We ask that your Holy Spirit would continue to push us toward repentance, for we know that there is great freedom to be found there. We love you, Father, and thank you for Jesus. Amen

RECONCILIATION

Reconciliation focuses on restoring broken relationships between an offender and the offended. In *He's My Brother*, John Perkins shares the story of his reconciliation with a member of the Ku Klux Klan.[5]

In Africa, we have seen the hard work of reconciliation in Rwanda, where for decades the Hutus and Tutsis were at odds with each other. This resulted in what we have come to know as the Rwandan Genocide. Over twenty years later, there are hundreds of stories of reconciled relationships between Hutus and Tutsis.

In the Bible, the need for personal reconciliation is found in John 18 when Peter denies Jesus (as Jesus predicted). In John 21:15–25, Jesus reconciles Peter to Himself. During this process both parties have to be ready for reconciliation. Not everyone wants or is ready for restored relationships.

Reconciliation, unlike forgiveness, cannot be one-sided. It takes genuine repentance to pursue reconciliation. Confession plus repentance can lead to reconciliation.

Discussion Questions:

- How do we use the ministry of reconciliation in our racial divisions?

- How does our being reconciled to Christ relate to our being reconciled to each other?

- What does it mean to be an ambassador for Christ?

- How do we move from forgiveness to reconciliation?

- How are people reconciled to Christ? How can we be used in reconciling people to Christ?

- Pray and ask God to show you broken relationships that need mending. Write the person's name down. Ask God to create an opportunity to pursue reconciliation.

The church and its people need to be credible witnesses for the unity we find in Christ. Our reconciliation to Christ should cause us to be reconciled to one another in such a way that relationships damaged by sin are restored. As the body of Christ, we must not ignore racial issues—whether personal or systemic. Our goal should be to see the church at work in a process of the restoration of relationships. As ambassadors of

Christ, we need to take part in "making things right." Reconciliation is the fruit of confession, repentance and forgiveness. We Christians must take an active role in helping to bring unity to the world.

Prayer:

> Father, help us to reflect the essence of who You are by the way we treat one another. We are heartbroken about the brokenness we see around us. We know You are the remedy for the brokenness that we see in our world. Continue to show us the places in our hearts that need healing from prejudices, assumptions and fears. Guide us in removing barriers that hinder us from becoming all You created us to be. Help us to become beacons that will penetrate the darkness of the world we live in. We know that Your grace can transform our hearts to make us one. We pray that the world may see that—for Your glory. In Jesus name, Amen.

Amen and amen. That was how Tenth's own Reconcilers' Fellowship ended each of our sessions—in prayer—with each member sharing his or her brokenness and need for God's grace to live together with the servant heats that are required of good neighbors.

WEB RESOURCES

Active Compassion:
http://www.activecompassion.org/index.php?section=home&page=home

Biblical Guidelines for Mercy Ministry:
http://www.pcahistory.org/pca/2-414.html

Christian Community Development Association: www.ccda.org

Diaconal Ministries Canada, partner of the Christian Reformed Church in North America: www.diaconalministries.com

Faith & Service Technical Education Network (FASTEN): www.fastennetwork.org

Presbyterian Church in America, Mission to North America: www.pcamna.org

Tenth Presbyterian Church: www.tenth.org

BOOKS

Larry Crabb and Dan Allender: *Encouragement: The Key to Caring*

David S. Apple: *Not Just a Soup Kitchen*

Gerard Berghoef and Lester DeKoster: *The Deacons Handbook*

Steve Corbett and Brian Fikkert: *When Helping Hurts; Helping Without Hurting in Church Benevolence*

Kenneth Haugk: *Christian Caregiving: A Way of Life*

Timothy J. Keller: *Ministries of Mercy; Resources for Deacons*

James R. Kok: *90% of Helping is Just Showing Up*

Robert D. Lupton: *Toxic Charity*

Randy Nabors: *Merciful*

Henri Nouwen: *Compassion: A Reflection on the Christian Life*

John Perkins: *Beyond Charity*

Andrew Purves: *The Search for Compassion*

Ronald J. Sider, Philip N. Olson and Heidi Rolland Unruh: *Churches That Make a Difference*

Amy L. Sherman: *Restorers of Hope*

Chris Sicks: *Tangible*

Alexander Strauch: *The New Testament Deacon*

Jay Van Groningen: *Changing Times, New Approaches: Handbook for Deacons*

Lori Wiersma and Connie Kuiper VanDyke: *Deacon's Handbook*

NOTES

INTRODUCTION

1. Tenth Presbyterian Church, accessed September 10, 2016, http://www.tenth.org/about/sundays-at-tenth.
2. David S. Apple, *Not Just a Soup Kitchen: How Mercy Ministry in the Local Church Transforms Us All* (Fort Washington, PA: CLC Publications, 2014).

CHAPTER 1: A THEOLOGY OF CARING

1. James Bryan Smith, *A Spiritual Formation Workbook: Small Group Resources for Nurturing Christian Growth* (San Francisco: HarperCollins, 1991), 21.
2. Larry Crabb and Dan Allender, *Encouragement: The Key to Caring* (Grand Rapids: Zondervan Publishing, 1984), 80.
3. Henri J.M. Nouwen, *Reaching Out: The Three Movements of the Spiritual Life* (New York: Image Books, 1975), 27.
4. Ibid., 87.
5. Ibid., 89.
6. Ibid.
7. Dallas Willard, *The Spirit of the Disciplines: Understanding How God Changes Lives* (San Francisco: Harper and Row, 1988), 182.
8. Richard J. Foster, *Celebration of Discipline: The Path to Spiritual Growth* (New York: Harper and Row, 1978), 112.
9. Ibid., 112–113.
10. Adelaide A. Pollard, "Have Thine Own Way, Lord," *Trinity Hymnal* (Suwanee, GA: Great Commission Publications, 1991), 726.

11. Nouwen, *Reaching Out,* 66.

12. Andrew Purves, *The Search for Compassion: Spirituality and Ministry* (Louisville: John Knox Press, 1989), 35.

13. Ibid., 124.

14. Ibid., 131.

CHAPTER 2: DEVELOPING THE HEART OF A SERVANT

1. William Barclay, Commentary on Matthew 16:24-26, *William Barclay's Daily Study Bible* (1956-1959), accessed October 12, 2016, http://www.studylight. org/ commentaries/dsb/matthew-16.html; William Barclay, Commentary on Luke 9:23-27, *William Barclay's Daily Study Bible* (1956-1959), accessed October 12, 2016, http://www.studylight.org/commentaries/dsb/luke-9.html.

2. Matthew Henry, Complete Commentary on Matthew 16:24-28, *Matthew Henry Complete Commentary on the Whole Bible* (1706), accessed October 12, 2016, http://www.studylight.org/commentaries/mhm/matthew-16.html.

3. *Baker's Evangelical Dictionary of Biblical Theology,* s.v. "denial," accessed September 15, 2016, http://www.biblestudytools.com/dictionaries/bakers-evangelical-dictionary/denial.html.

4. Gerald W. Schlabach, *And Who Is My Neighbor? Poverty, Privilege, and the Gospel of Christ* (Scottdale, PA: Herald Press, 1990), 25.

5. Dietrich Bonhoeffer, *The Cost of Discipleship* (New York: Macmillan, 1963), 47–48.

6. Ibid., 98.

7. Ibid., vii.

8. Kosuke Koyama, *Waterbuffalo Theology* (Maryknoll, NY: Orbis Books), 25.

9. Bonhoeffer, *The Cost of Discipleship,* 84.

10. C. John Miller, *Outgrowing the Ingrown Church* (Grand Rapids: Zondervan Publishing, 1982), 84.

11. Ibid., 154.

12. Ernest Hollings, quoted in Thomas E. Ludwig et al., eds., *Inflation, Poortalk and the Gospel* (Valley Forge, PA: Judson Press, 1981), 72.

13. Flavius Josephus, The Second Book of the Wars of the jews, 610, accessed December 21, 2016, http://quod.lib.umich.edu/e/eebo/A46286.0001.001/1:2 4?rgn=div1;view=fulltext.

14. *Word Biblical Commentary,* Donald A. Hagner, vol. 33b, *Matthew* 14-28 (Dallas: Word Books, 1995), 483.

15. James M. Boice and Philip G. Ryken, *The Heart of the Cross* (Wheaton: Crossway Books, 1999), 181.

16. Ibid.

17. David Hagopian, "Trading Places: The Priesthood of All Believers," Center for Reformed Theology and Apologetics, accessed September 15, 2016, http://www. reformed.org/webfiles/antithesis/index.html?mainframe=/ webfiles/antithesis/ v1n3/ant_v1n3_record.html.

18. Cyril Eastwood, *The Priesthood of All Believers: An Examination of the Doctrine from the Reformation to the Present Day* (Eugene: Wipf and Stock Publishers, 2009), 12.

19. Adolph Spaeth et al., trans. and eds., "A Treatise on Good Works" in *Works of Martin Luther* (Philadelphia: A.J. Holman Co., 1915), accessed September 15, 2016, http://www.iclnet.org/pub/resources/text/wittenberg/luther/work-02a.txt.

20. *The Belgic Confession* (1991 Translation), Article 24, "The Sanctification of Sinners," accessed September 15, 2016, https://www.rca.org/resources/belgic-confession.

21. Spaeth et al., "A Treatise on Good Works."

22. Greg Ogden, *The New Reformation: Returning the Ministry to the People of God* (Grand Rapids: Zondervan Publishing, 1990), 12.

23. Koyama, *Waterbuffalo Theology,* 107.

24. Gerard Berghoef and Lester DeKoster, *The Deacons Handbook: A Manual of Stewardship* (Grand Rapids: Christian's Library Press, 1980), 215.

25. Anthony J. Carter, *Blood Work: How the Blood of Christ Accomplishes Our Salvation* (Sanford, FL: Reformation Trust Publishing, 2013), 105.

26. Richard J. Mouw, *Called to Holy Worldliness* (Philadelphia: Fortress Press, 1980), 88.

CHAPTER 3: A NATION OF GIVERS

1. John Winthrop, quoted in Brian O'Connell, *America's Voluntary Spirit: A Book of Readings* (New York: Foundation Center, 1983), 32.

2. Ibid.

3. Alexis de Tocqueville, *Democracy in America* (New York: Vintage, 1945), 2.

4. Ray Bakke, *A Theology as Big as the City* (Downers Grove: InterVarsity Press, 1997), 61.

5. Robert Wuthnow, *Acts of Compassion: Caring for Others and Helping Ourselves* (Princeton: Princeton University Press, 1993), 10-11.

6. Richard A. Kauffman, "Beyond Bake Sales: Christian Volunteerism Needs to Be Directed Toward the Deepest Hurts," *Christianity Today,* June 16, 1997, 12.

7. Michael Gerson, "Do Do-Gooders Do Much Good?" *U.S. News & World Report,* April 28, 1997.

8. Kauffman, "Beyond Bake Sales," 13.

9. Roberto Rivera, quoted in Kauffman, "Beyond Bake Sales," 13.

10. Gerson, "Do Do-Gooders Do Much Good?"

11. Wuthnow, *Acts of Compassion,* 25.

12. Albert Schweitzer, quoted in Wuthnow, *Acts of Compassion,* 65.

13. Wuthnow, *Acts of Compassion,* 101-102.

14. Timothy J. Keller, *Ministries of Mercy: The Call of the Jericho Road* (Grand Rapids: Zondervan Publishing, 1989), 108.

CHAPTER 4: LISTENING

1. I have adapted this conversation with permission from the author. It appears in Ben Vandezande's out of print book, *Servant Leaders: A Practical Guide for Deacons* (Grand Rapids, CRC Publications, 2000), 18. The comments and critique of the conversation are mine.

2. Thomas T. Waggoner, "Never Heard of 'Em," *Claude (TX) News,* August 4, 1944, The Portal to Texas History, accessed February 19, 2016, https://texashistory.unt.edu/ark:/67531/metapth353787/m1/9/?q=never%20heard%20of%20%27em.

CHAPTER 6: THE CHURCH AT WORK

1. "Of Good Works," chap. 26.2 in *The Westminster Confession of Faith,* Center for Reformed Theology and Apologetics, accessed September 16, 2016, http://www.reformed.org/documents/wcf_with_ proofs/.

2. James M. Boice, *Philippians: An Expositional Commentary* (Nashville: Zondervan Publishing, 1982).

3. Edward T. Welch, *Side by Side: Walking with Others in Wisdom and Love* (Wheaton: Crossway Books, 2015), 12-13.

4. Pat Ennis and Lisa Tatlock, *Practicing Hospitality: The Joy of Serving Others* (Wheaton: Crossway Books, 2008), 237-238.

5. James M. Boice, *The Gospel of Matthew* (Grand Rapids: Baker Books, 2001), 535; James M. Boice, *Romans: The New Humanity,* vol 4 (Grand Rapids: Baker Book House, 1991), 1743.

CHAPTER 7: VISITATION

1. Amy L. Sherman, *Sharing God's Heart for the Poor: Meditations for Worship, Prayer and Service* (Charlottesville: Trinity Presbyterian Church, 2000), 17.

CHAPTER 8: SHEPHERDING

1. Phillip Keller, *A Shepherd Looks at Psalm 23* (Grand Rapids: Zondervan Publishing, 1970), 29.
2. Ibid., 31.
3. Ibid., 36.
4. Ibid., 37.
5. Ibid., 43.
6. Ibid., 46.
7. Ibid., 50.
8. Ibid., 62.
9. Ibid., 62-63.
10. Ibid., 66.

CHAPTER 9: LISTENING REVISITED

1. Richard Rodgers and Oscar Hammerstein II, "You've Got to Be Carefully Taught," on *South Pacific,* Columbia Records, 1950.
2. Susan M. Glisson and April Grayson, "The Children Shall Lead," Freedom Riders documentary, Winter Institute, 2005, accessed September 9, 2016, vimeo. com/70196633.
3. Stan Vander Klay, *Chains of Grace* (Charleston: Booksurge Publishing 2005), 44-45.
4. Christena Cleveland, "What Story Will You Tell," from a message presented at Urbana Student Missions Conference, St. Louis, MO, December 2015, accessed September 16, 2016, https://urbana.org/message/christena-cleveland.
5. Thom and Marcia Hopler, *Reaching the World Next Door: How to Spend the Gospel in the Midst of Many Cultures* (Downers Grove: InterVarsity Press, 1978), 188.
6. Spencer Perkins and Chris Rice, *More Than Equals: Racial Healing for the Sake of the Gospel* (Downers Grove, InterVarsity Press, 1996), 148, 189-190).

7. Video series is based on Dr. Tony Evans' book, *Let's Get to Know Each Other: What White and Black Christians Need to Know about Each Other* (Nashville: Thomas Nelson Publishers, 1995).

8. Carl F. Ellis Jr, *Free at Last? The Gospel in the African-American Experience* (Downers Grove: InterVarsity Press, 1996).

9. Ibid., 80.

10. Nouwen, *Reaching Out*, 66.

11. Latasha Morrison, "Racial Unity Guide," accessed November 23, 2016, http://beabridgebuilder.com/wp-content/uploads/2016/02/racial-unity-edited.pdf. Adapted and used by permission.

12. Margery Williams, *The Velveteen Rabbit* (New York: Henry Holt and Company, 1983), 4.

CHAPTER 10: DEVELOPING HEALTHY BOUNDARIES IN THE BODY OF CHRIST

1. Christine Guth, "Healthy Boundaries in the Body of Christ," Anabaptist Disabilities Network, October 2008, http://www.adnetonline.org/SiteCollectionDocuments/Healthy-Boundaries-in-the-Body-of-Christ.pdf. Adapted and used by permission.

2. Ibid.

3. Bill Gaultiere, "Jesus Set Boundaries," Soul Shepherding, July 20, 1998, http://www.soulshepherding.org/1998/07/jesus-set-boundaries. Adapted and used by permission.

APPENDIX: ADDITIONAL TOOLS AND RESOURCES

1. Morrison, "Racial Unity Guide."

2. John R.W. Stott, *Confess Your Sins: The Way of Reconciliation* (Dallas: Word Books, 1974).

3. Martin Luther King Jr., "Quotable Quotes," Goodreads, accessed September 19, 2016, http://www.goodreads.com/quotes/57037-forgiveness-is-not-an-occasional-act-it-is-a-constant.

4. A.W. Tozer, *Man—the Dwelling Place of God: What It Means to Have Christ Living in You* (Camp Hill, PA: WingSpread Publishers, 2008).

5. John Perkins and Thomas A. Tarrants III, *He's My Brother: Former Racial Foes Offer Strategy for Reconciliation* (Grand Rapids: Baker Publishing, 1994).

BIBLIOGRAPHY

Apple, David S. *Not Just a Soup Kitchen: How Mercy Ministry in the Local Church Transforms Us All.* Fort Washington, PA: CLC Publications, 2014.

Bakers Evangelical Dictionary of Biblical Theology. http://www.biblestudytools.com/dictionaries/bakers-evangelical-dictionary.

Bakke, Ray. *A Theology as Big as the City.* Downers Grove: InterVarsity Press. 1997.

Barclay, William. *The Daily Bible Study Series.* rev. ed. Colorado Springs: NavPress, 1995.

Beattie, Melody. *Codependent No More.* San Francisco: Harper and Row, 1987.

Berghoef, Gerard, and Lester DeKoster. *The Deacons Handbook: A Manual of Stewardship.* Grand Rapids: Christian's Library Press, 1980.

Birkey, Verna. *Women Connecting with Women.* Enumclaw: Winepress Publishing, 1998.

Boice, James M. *Philippians: An Expositional Commentary.* Nashville: Zondervan Publishing, 1982.

Boice, James M., and Philip G. Ryken. *The Heart of the Cross.* Wheaton: Crossway Books, 1999.

Bonhoeffer, Dietrich. *The Cost of Discipleship.* New York: Macmillan, 1963.

Burlingame, Gary. *Crossing the Bridges God Builds.* Golden, CO: Healthy Life Press, 2015.

Calvin, John. *The Institutes of the Christian Religion.* Philadelphia: Westminster Press, 1960.

Carter, Anthony J. *Blood Work: How the Blood of Christ Accomplishes Our Salvation.* Sanford, FL: Reformation Trust Publishing, 2013.

Clapper, Gregory. *As if the Heart Mattered.* Nashville: The Upper Room, 1997.

Cloud, Henry, and John Townsend. *Boundaries.* Grand Rapids: Zondervan, 1992.

Cloud, Henry, and John Townsend. *Boundaries with Kids.* Grand Rapids: Zondervan, 1998.

Crabb, Larry, and Dan Allender. *Encouragement: The Key to Caring.* Grand Rapids: Zondervan Publishing, 1984.

de Tocqueville, Alexis. *Democracy in America.* New York: Vintage, 1945.

DeYoung, Curtiss Paul. *Reconciliation: Our Greatest Challenge, Our Only Hope.* King of Prussia, PA: Judson Press, 1997.

Eastwood, Cyril. *The Priesthood of All Believers: An Examination of the Doctrine from the Reformation to the Present Day.* Eugene: Wipf and Stock Publishers, 2009.

Edwards, Jefferson. *Purging Racism from Christianity: Freedom & Purpose.* Nashville: Zondervan Publishing, 1996.

Ellis, Carl F., Jr. *Free at Last? The Gospel in the African-American Experience.* Downers Grove: InterVarsity Press, 1996.

Ennis, Pat, and Lisa Tatlock. *Practicing Hospitality: The Joy of Serving Others.* Wheaton: Crossway Books, 2008.

Foster, Richard J. *Celebration of Discipline: The Path to Spiritual Growth.* New York: Harper and Row, 1978.

Gaultiere, Bill. "Jesus Set Boundaries." Soul Shepherding. July 20, 1998. http://www.soulshepherding.org/1998/07/jesus-set-boundaries.

Gerson, Michael. "Do Do-Gooders Do Much Good?" *U.S. News & World Report.* April 28, 1997.

Glisson, Susan M., and April Grayson. "The Children Shall Lead," Freedom Riders documentary. Winter Institute, 2005. vimeo.com/70196633.

Greider, Kathleen. *Much Madness Is Divinest Sense.* Cleveland: Pilgrim Press, 2007.

Guth, Christine. "Healthy Boundaries in the Body of Christ." Anabaptist Disabilities Network. October 2008. http://www.adnetonline.org/SiteCollectionDocuments/Healthy-Boundaries-in-the-Body-of-Christ.pdf.

Hagner, Donald A. *Word Biblical Commentary.* Vol. 33b, *Matthew* 14-28. Dallas: Word Books, 1995.

Hagopian, David. "Trading Places: The Priesthood of All Believers." http://www.reformed.org/webfiles/antithesis/index.html?mainframe=/webfiles/antithesis/v1n3/ant_v1n3_record.html.

Harmon, Willis. *An Incomplete Guide to the Future.* New York: W.W. Norton, 1970.

Henry, Matthew, *Commentaries on the Bible.* Colorado Springs: NavPress, 1995.

Hopler, Thom, and Marcia. *Reaching the World Next Door: How to Spend the Gospel in the Midst of Many Cultures.* Downers Grove: InterVarsity Press, 1978.

Kauffman, Richard A. "Beyond Bake Sales: Christian Volunteerism Needs to be Directed Toward the Deepest Hurts." *Christianity Today.* June 16, 1997.

Keller, Phillip. *A Shepherd Looks at Psalm 23.* Grand Rapids: Zondervan Publishing, 1970.

Keller, Timothy J. *Ministries of Mercy: The Call of the Jericho Road.* Grand Rapids: Zondervan Publishing, 1989.

Koyama, Kosuke. *Waterbuffalo Theology.* Maryknoll: Orbis Books, 1974.

Linehan, Marsha. *Skills Training Manual for Treating Borderline Personality Disorder.* New York: Guilford Press, 1993.

Ludwig, Thomas E., Merold Wesphal, Robin Klay, and David G. Meyers, eds. *Inflation, Poortalk and the Gospel.* Valley Forge, PA: Judson Press, 1981.

McCord, James I., and T. H. L. Parker, eds. *Service in Christ: Essays presented to Karl Barth on his Eightieth Birthday.* Grand Rapids: Eerdmans Publishing, 1966.

Miller, C. John. *Outgrowing the Ingrown Church.* Grand Rapids: Zondervan Publishing, 1982.

Mouw, Richard J. *Called to Holy Worldliness.* Philadelphia: Fortress Press, 1980.

Nouwen, Henri J.M. *Reaching Out: The Three Movements of the Spiritual Life.* New York: Image Books, 1975.

O'Connell, Brian. *America's Voluntary Spirit: A Book of Readings.* New York: Foundation Center, 1983.

Ogden, Greg. *The New Reformation: Returning the Ministry to the People of God.* Grand Rapids: Zondervan Publishing, 1990.

Patterson, Ben. "Noble Volunteer or Humble Slave?" *Leadership: A Practical Journal for Church Leaders* 3, no. 3 (Summer 1982).

Perkins, Spencer, and Chris Rice. *More Than Equals: Racial Healing for the Sake of the Gospel.* Downers Grove: InterVarsity Press, 1996.

Pollard, Adelaide A. "Have Thine Own Way, Lord." Trinity Hymnal. Suwanee, GA: Great Commission Publications, 1991.

Purves, Andrew. *The Search for Compassion: Spirituality and Ministry.* Louisville: John Knox Press, 1989.

Ray, Veronica. *Setting Boundaries.* Center City, MN: Hazelden Publishing, 1989.

Rodgers, Richard, and Oscar Hammerstein II, "You've Got to be Carefully Taught" on *South Pacific.* Columbia Records. Recorded 1950.

Qubein, Nido. "How to Avoid Communication Barriers." http://www.nidoqubein. com/articles/40/How To Avoid Communication Barriers.

Schlabach, Gerald W. *And Who Is My Neighbor? Poverty, Privilege, and the Gospel of Christ.* Scottdale, PA: Herald Press, 1990.

Sherman, Amy L. *Sharing God's Heart for the Poor: Meditations for Worship, Prayer and Service.* Charlottesville: Trinity Presbyterian Church, 2000.

Smith, James Bryan. *A Spiritual Formation Workbook: Small Group Resources for Nurturing Christian Growth.* San Francisco: HarperCollins, 1991.

Snyder, Howard. *Radical Renewal: The Problem with Wineskins Today.* Houston: Touch Publications, 1996.

Spaeth, Adolph, L.D. Reed, Henry Eyster Jacobs, et al., trans. and eds. "A Treatise on Good Works" in *Works of Martin Luther.* Philadelphia: A.J. Holman Co., 1915.

Stevens, J. Paul. *The Equippers Guide for Church Ministry.* Downers Grove: InterVarsity Press, 1985.

Stott, John R.W. *Confess Your Sins: The Way of Reconciliation.* Dallas: Word Books, 1974.

Stull, Terry. *The Disease of Racism: Rediscovering the Cure.* Companion Press, 1996.

Vandezande, Ben. *Servant Leaders: A Practical Guide for Deacons.* Grand Rapids: CRC Publications, 2000.

Vander Klay, Stanley. *Chains of Grace.* Charleston: Booksurge Publishing, 2005.

Van Klinken, Jaap. *Diakonia: Mutual Helping with Justice and Compassion.* Grand Rapids: Eerdmans Publishing, 1989.

Waggoner, Thomas T. "Never Heard of 'Em." *Claude (TX) News.* August 4, 1944. https://texashistory.unt.edu/ark:/67531/metapth353787/m1/9/?q=never%20heard%20of%20%27em.

Welch, Edward T. *Side by Side: Walking with Others in Wisdom and Love.* Wheaton: Crossway Books, 2015.

Willard, Dallas. *The Spirit of the Disciplines: Understanding How God Changes Lives*. San Francisco: Harper and Row, 1988.

Williams, Margery. *The Velveteen Rabbit*. New York: Henry Holt and Company, 1983.

Wuthnow, Robert. *Acts of Compassion: Caring for Others and Helping Ourselves*. Princeton: Princeton University Press, 1993.

PUBLICATIONS

Fort Washington, PA 19034

This book is published by CLC Publications, an outreach of CLC Ministries International. The purpose of CLC is to make evangelical Christian literature available to all nations so that people may come to faith and maturity in the Lord Jesus Christ. We hope this book has been life changing and has enriched your walk with God through the work of the Holy Spirit. If you would like to know more about CLC, we invite you to visit our website:

www.clcusa.org

To know more about the remarkable story of the founding of CLC International we encourage you to read

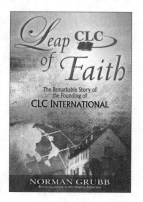

LEAP OF FAITH

Norman Grubb

Paperback
Size 5¹/₄ x 8, Pages 248
ISBN: 978-0-87508-650-7
ISBN (*e-book*): 978-1-61958-055-8

NOT JUST A SOUP KITCHEN

Dr. David S. Apple

Not Just a Soup Kitchen is the story of how God transformed
the life of the author from near-death skull fracture, childhood
sexual abuse, and spiritual bankruptcy to becoming the minister
of mercy in the heart of Philadelphia. It is also an instructional
guide for those serving in diaconal/mercy ministries.

Paperback
Size 5¹/₄ x 8, Pages 255
ISBN: 978-1-61958-174-6
ISBN (*e-book*): 978-1-61958-175-3

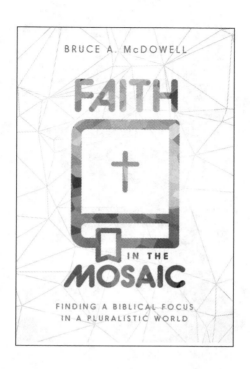

FAITH IN THE MOSAIC

Bruce A. McDowell

We live in a pluralistic age—and we come into contact with people from different faith traditions on a daily basis. This context challenges our faith. How should we, as Christians, think about those outside of our faith? Are we the only ones who are right? How do we know? Bruce McDowell's *Faith in the Mosaic* will help you wade through those questions.

Paperback
Size 5¹/₄ x 8, Pages 324
ISBN: 978-1-61958-247-7
ISBN (*e-book*): 978-1-61958-248-4